Handbook
of
Narcotics
Control

Prentice-Hall
Essentials of Law Enforcement Series

James D. Stinchcomb
Series Editor

Handbook of Narcotics Control

DENNY F. PACE

JIMMIE C. STYLES
Vice Chancellor,
Tarrant County Junior College
Fort Worth, Texas

PRENTICE-HALL, INC.
Englewood Cliffs, New Jersey

ISBN: P-0-13-380469-0
        C-0-13-380477-1
Library of Congress Card Catalog Number: 75-37962
Printed in the United States of America

10 9 8 7 6 5 4 3 2 1

PRENTICE-HALL INTERNATIONAL, INC., *London*
PRENTICE-HALL OF AUSTRALIA, PTY. LTD., *Sydney*
PRENTICE-HALL OF CANADA, LTD., *Toronto*
PRENTICE-HALL OF INDIA PRIVATE LIMITED, *New Delhi*
PRENTICE-HALL OF JAPAN, INC., *Tokyo*

Introduction

Surely nothing can be more fundamental to guaranteeing the delivery of professional services than the employment of properly trained personnel. In pursuit of that goal, law enforcement officers and those who train them have long recognized the need for concise yet thoroughly documented information, well-researched and accurately presented.

In recent years, several commendable efforts have resulted in the availability of some valuable training resources. But too few of these were professionally developed by the textbook publishing companies, although their assistance was becoming imperative. The Prentice-Hall Essentials of Law Enforcement Series has been developed following a conference of national authorities who were asked to determine topics for priority production. The subject areas chosen are both timely and critical to the police and to their own increased determination to improve their service.

The potential use for this series is limited only by the creative imaginations of those responsible for peace officers' access to learning. Each book may perform as a supplement to a college course, as a resource for a training program, or as a reader to encourage informal study. It is the hope and the intent of the publisher, the editor, and the authors that these practical texts will contribute to the continuing progress being achieved by the nation's police.

James D. Stinchcomb

Virginia Commonwealth University

Preface

The role of law enforcement toward problems of drug abuse has three dimensions: first, to assist in the educational effort of all social agencies; second, to assist the drug abuser with referral to hospitals and agencies that may effect rehabilitation and third, to make physical arrests when other efforts have failed to successfully cope with drug abuse problems as they are encountered.

This handbook is an attempt to assist the field officer in understanding the importance of drug control problems in a manner which incorporates these three dimensions. The major emphasis here is on the third aspect, since law enforcement is charged with enforcing the statutory provisions of each state. Punitive law enforcement is carried on with full knowledge that education and rehabilitation cannot resolve the problem of the "hard-core" addict nor can the professional drug peddler be discouraged by any method other than punitive isolation.

With full acknowledgment of other more humane ways of dealing with the drug problem, this handbook is written so that the field officer can rely upon procedures that are effective, lawful, and logical in his daily enforcement efforts.

Contents

APPENDIX II

Contents

Handbook
of
Narcotics
Control

An Overview of the Drug Abuse Problem

Enforcement is only one phase of the many social and legal processes developed to control excessive drug abuse. Enforcement is an important phase primarily because it is the process employed after all other methods of prevention have failed. Since punitive enforcement is the last-resort process, it is important for the enforcement officer to know why, as well as how, he should enforce drug laws. In order to help an officer identify his limited role in drug enforcement, we begin with an overview of some aspects of current knowledge and research in the field of drug abuse. The emphasis is on (1) justification for the enforcement of drug laws; (2) general trends in drug control in the United States; and (3) expert opinions on drug abuse in society.

Justification for the Enforcement of Drug Laws

The officer's involvement in enforcement of drug laws is much like his involvement in enforcement of other laws dealing with vice crimes. There is strong public and professional pressure to legalize certain prohibited drugs and to handle users as medical problems rather than as criminals. The role of the police is to cooperate in and support any program that can help alleviate the problem. Until programs other than punitive enforcement are created by legislation and are developed, the enforcement officer is mandated to take legal action on each violation and has no alternative but to take enforcement action for violations of existing statutes.

Halting traffic in illegal drugs is an international problem.

chapter

1

Organizations such as the United Nations and Interpol, as well as various departments of the United States and foreign governments, are involved in the suppression and eradication of drug traffic. When these international and national efforts fail, state and local enforcement moves in, and is faced with a problem with which it is poorly equipped to deal effectively.

There does not appear to be a *best* way to prevent drug availability or abuse. Education, sociological prevention, psychological treatment, and punitive isolation are all techniques that have been used. Each technique has had a limited degree of success. Recognizing these limitations, this handbook addresses itself to the legal processes involving punitive isolation of the users and sellers of illegal drugs.

The processes of arrest and isolation involve considerable risk to the rights of individuals while protecting the rights of society. As with many traditions in the United States, the rights of society have frequently been reaffirmed in terms of more stringent laws, greater enforcement effort, and longer isolation of the violator. What has been overlooked by many people in law enforcement, in terms of its application to actual objective programs, is that punitive enforcement alone cannot succeed without a more logical attack upon the basic *causes* of drug abuse.

This paradox places the enforcement officer in a highly sensitive position, for abuses of liberal search and seizure laws may be sanctioned by such techniques as wiretap, electronic surveillance, and no-knock laws. By placing such powerful instruments in the hands of enforcement agencies, legislators have implied that the drug problem extends beyond the normal procedures of control and have empowered these agencies to use whatever means are necessary to reinstate a realistic and tolerable balance of control.

Law enforcement agencies dealing with drug enforcement are likely to find drug-control laws being abused unless officers possess both a moral responsibility and a high degree of legal knowledge, so that they can develop procedures that rigidly adhere to the *intent* of the law. The field officer must understand both the moral and the legal goals, and must develop links of assistance to achieve them.

There is no accurate way to predict or assess the number of drug users in the United States. However, estimates indicate that there are in excess of 75,000 hard-core addicts and perhaps as many as 180,000 heroin users. Figures for marihuana users approximate 8 to 10 million. Although law enforcement systems must deal with all the violators, emphasis in this hand-book is on the hard-core drug addict and the peddlers of all illegal drugs. Table One is cited to support the estimates given.

Table One
Arrest Data from the 1970 Uniform Crime Reports

1. Narcotic Drug Law arrests (yearly total)   415,000

2. Narcotic Drug Law arrests per 100,000 population:

Group I cities, 250,000+ population	393.1
Group II cities, 100,000 to 250,000 population	239.0
Group III cities, 50,000 to 100,000 population	229.0
Group IV cities, 25,000 to 50,000 population	177.6
Group V cities, 10,000 to 25,000 population	141.2
Group VI cities, 10,000 under population	115.5
Suburban areas	185.7
Rural areas	64.5
Total Population	228.5

3. Number of persons arrested for Narcotic Drug Laws in 1960 as compared with 1970.

	1960	1970	Percent Change
Total all ages	31,611	265,734	+740.6
Under 18 years of age	1,664	54,856	+3,196.6
18 years of age and over	20,947	220,878	+604.2

Taken from the Federal Bureau of Investigation, 1970 "Uniform Crime Reporter" (Washington, D.C.: Government Printing Office), pp. 119-130.

Early efforts in the United States to control narcotics traffic have evolved through the development and enforcement of the following legislation:

Federal Pure Food and Drug Act of 1906.
Harrison Narcotic Act of 1914. (This statute was a part of the Internal Revenue Act, designed to keep the entire process of drug distribution a matter of record. The tax on heroin was one cent per ounce.)
Narcotic Import and Export Act of 1922. (The domestic manufacture of heroin was outlawed in 1924.)
Marihuana Tax Act of 1937. (This statute was also a part of the Internal Revenue Act. The tax was $100 per ounce or fraction thereof on marihuana.)
Opium Poppy Control Act of 1942.

Justification for the Enforcement of Drug Laws

Boggs Act of 1951. (This act established more severe punishment for narcotic convictions.)
Narcotics Control Act of 1956.
Drug Abuse Laws of 1965.
Comprehensive Drug Abuse Prevention and Control Act of 1970. (See Appendixes 1 and 2.)

Since 1909 the United States has promoted treaties, protocols, and conventions in an effort to establish international controls on narcotic traffic. The Narcotic Control Board was established in 1922 to study national goals for the suppression of narcotics. These efforts, while not totally effective, have had some impact upon international drug sales and use.

A White House conference on "preventive measures for drug addiction" was called in 1962. This conference developed the guidelines for the Drug Abuse Control Act of 1965 and marked the beginning of a concentrated effort by national and local authorities to study and handle the rapidly growing problem of illegal drugs. The Omnibus Crime Bill of 1969 has given further impetus to the development of new approaches to the control of drug problems.

During the past two decades there have been several trends contributing to the drug enforcement problem. Some of them are cited from the 1970 Uniform Crime Reports.

1. Increased usage of narcotics and other dangerous drugs by younger persons—those who are between 18 and 30 years of age. In 1970 approximately 53 percent of the arrests for the narcotic drug laws were persons under 21 years of age.
2. Analysis of the 1970 Uniform Crime Reports indicates that 26 percent of the marihuana arrests were persons under the age of 18, and 62 percent of the arrests for marihuana involved persons under 21 years of age . . . females accounted for 16 percent of all narcotic drug arrests.[1]
3. Increased drug usage by socially and economically disadvantaged persons. Narcotic usage has often been called the crime of the poor, but in the past decade it has become a middle and upper class problem as well.
4. Increased usage by members of minority ethnic groups. (This trend is based on arrest figures and may be more indicative of arrest statistics than drug usage.)

[1] Federal Bureau of Investigation, *1970 Uniform Crime Reports* (Washington, D.C.: Government Printing Office).

5. Concentration of users in larger cities. This would apply to states where the major narcotic problems exist. New York has 50 percent of the nation's known narcotic addicts, Illinois has 13 percent, and California has 12 percent.[2] Available figures indicate that at least 80 percent of drug arrests are from metropolitan areas with populations greater than 3 million.
6. Increased and widespread consumption of different types of drugs. Drugs are being taken in pairs, or in combinations and ingested with alcoholic beverages. These addicts are often found to be suicides and contributors to highway fatalities.
7. Increased association of all drugs with crime. While there are statistics which argue both pro and con, most enforcement officers will attest to a high correlation between drug users and criminal activity.
8. Introduction of new drugs, and new types of drugs.[3]

In 1969 more than 13 billion pills were consumed. A large percentage of these pills were obtained through illegal sources. It has been pointed out that the sudden upsurge in the use of illicit drugs, chiefly the hallucinogenic and psychedelic types, may be due in part to:

1. Development of anti-intellectualism and an increase in mysticism.
2. Evangelism of the LSD experience, with "returning travelers" inviting one to "come over to LSD."
3. Sensationalism and exaggerated publicity.
4. The era of medicine for the mind, new insights into psychosomatic illnesses, with a strong reliance on the pallative effects of pills and medication.[4]

According to recent news reports, there are developments that are certain to have an impact on the national drug picture.

1. Turkey has agreed to ban all commercial cultivation of the opium poppy.

[2]Federal Bureau of Narcotics and Drug Abuse, *Fact Sheet No. 5* (Washington, D.C.: Government Printing Office, 1969) p. 5-1.

[3]Tunis E. Cordill, District Director, Public Health Social Work, Torrance District, Los Angeles County Health Department. Speech at California State College, Long Beach, October 22, 1966.

[4]Taken from a handout sheet entitled "Some Guidelines for the Proper Use of Psychedelic Chemicals." Author not identified. This document had wide distribution in the Southern California beach areas during 1967-68.

Justification for the Enforcement of Drug Laws

2. Middle eastern countries, chiefly Iran, have begun to impose the death penalty for possession of illegal narcotics. This should have an impact upon the shipment of drugs across international borders and the bootlegging of domestic narcotic production in these countries.
3. Increased cooperation between Mexico and the United States. This should help sever many of the thousands of illegal supply routes.
4. Increases in the staffs of federal agencies that maintain intelligence contacts in foreign countries.
5. The rapid development of international intelligence, aided in part by electronic data processing systems.
6. Increased surveillance of check points maintained by the United States Customs Service and the Border Patrol.
7. Better feedback to local agencies from a national intelligence system.
8. Mexico, Turkey, France, and the United States have signed a treaty agreeing to cooperate in controlling narcotics. Three million dollars has been loaned to Turkey to shift land to other crops and eradicate the planting of opium.
9. The United States Office of Education will train 150,000 teachers in the best ways of explaining drug dangers.

Expert Opinions on Drug Abuse in Society

Drug abuse has many contributing causes. Three of the most general causes are briefly identified as economic, sociological, and psychological. All of these can contribute to breakdowns in the system of criminal justice. The dominance of organized crime in drug traffic is one of the major economic factors and a significant reason why enforcement agencies cannot hope to completely control drug traffic at the local level.

Organized Crime and Drug Traffic

Most "hard narcotics" and marihuana are brought into the United States through tightly structured organized confederations. The structure extends from the apex of the hierarchy down to street level deliveries. Street deliveries are made by expendable "mules," but the planning, financing, and arranging for the length of sentence if a pusher is apprehended has already been developed and determined by the organization. Even natural family members carrying drugs from Mexico into the United States as a

An Overview of the Drug Abuse Problem

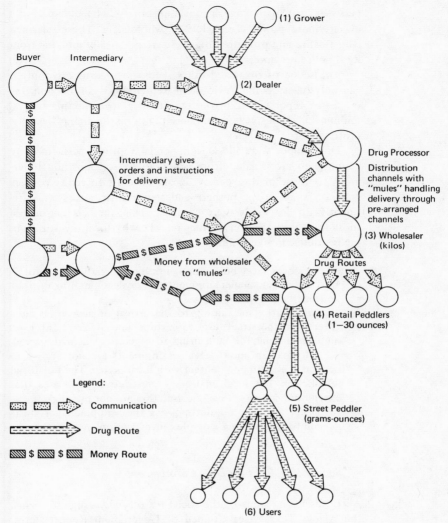

(1) Grower

Buyer   Intermediary

(2) Dealer

Intermediary gives
orders and instructions
for delivery

Drug Processor

Distribution
channels with
"mules" handling
delivery through
pre-arranged
channels

(3) Wholesaler
(kilos)

Money from wholesaler
to "mules"

Drug Routes

(4) Retail Peddlers
(1–30 ounces)

Legend:

⊡ ⊡ ⇨ Communication

⇨ Drug Route

$ $ $ Money Route

(5) Street Peddler
(grams-ounces)

(6) Users

1. Commercial and small growers sell to the dealers in raw materials (opium)

2. Buyer uses intermediary to contact dealer who arranges for processing and distribution.
    A token payment may change hands.

3. Intermediary carries orders and instructions for deliveries. Wholesaler has "mule" deliver to
    pre-arranged location. Sample is tested and buyer has "mule" make payoff to pre-arranged location.

4. Retail peddlers are contacted by the wholesaler with "mules" making all deliveries and contacts.
    Communications downward. Retailer sends money by "mule" to intermediary.

5. Street peddler is contacted by the retail peddlers. Street peddler then deals with the user.
    Communications both upward and downward.

Figure 1.1.   Drug sale procedures from grower to user.

Expert Opinions on Drug Abuse in Society

personal favor to an uncle, a cousin, or other kin become part of a bigger, more powerful echelon of wholesalers. These salesmen who finance and promote drug trade are practically immune from local police pressure.

The scope of organized crime's control of drug distribution can only be estimated. A House of Representatives subcommittee on crime reports that marihuana trade alone amounts to 850 million dollars per year.[5] And heroin, not marihuana, is the most profitable drug.

Drug imports are illegal commercial ventures performed by people who are isolated from others in the organizational hierarchy. Because of this secrecy, local police are forced to concentrate on small street pushers and minor distributors who frequently do not know their suppliers. This, then, is the end of most local investigations. Other reasons why local investigations are restrictive in scope are:

At the local level bulk shipments have already been broken into dozens of smaller shipments for dealers handling medium and small amounts.

Information pertaining to the arrival of new drugs must filter from the street level to enforcement officers. This gives additional time for bulk drugs to be concealed or dispersed.

Information about sizeable shipments are not known to persons who come in contact with local police. The territorial jurisdiction for local officers is restrictive and cases that extend outside an officer's jurisdiction are not pursued.

Local agencies do not possess the equipment or staffs needed to sustain long, complex investigations.

Sociological Basis for Drug Enforcement

In discussing some of the social reasons why drug use begins, the Alamo Texas Area Council of Government Report states:

... Most persons are initiated into the use of drugs by association with friends or acquaintances ... Persons start experimenting with drugs out of curiosity ... and ultimately to conform to expectations of their group. Teenagers fear not belonging to their peer group ... thus, teenagers use drugs

[5] First Report by the Select Committee on Crime, *Marihuana*, 91st Congress, 2nd Session, House Report No. 91-978 (Washington, D.C.: Government Printing Office, 1970) p. 19.

because others are doing it . . . To be like others is important for the adolescent group . . . Nothing is quite so insidious as the drug-using peer group.

Other reasons cited by this report are:

. . . Some adolescents in slum areas take drugs for the "kick," as something to heighten the present moment . . . Another of the "whys" of drug use involves the social customs that have grown up around drug use . . . In areas where the discrepancy between the "culture goals" and the "institution means" is greatest, condition of "anomie" prevails . . . Some traditional delinquents are so frustrated by not being able to achieve success that they retreat . . .[6]

In a report on drugs, The Interagency Council on Drug Abuse made numerous observations about drug abuse as a social problem. Some people argue that a drug user affects only himself and should not be harassed by other members of society. Can society determine whether or not an appreciable number of people can maintain drug habits without adversely affecting the lives of others?[7]

There is a good deal of support for the argument that excessive drug usage by the individual is detrimental to all society. Most experts agree that the psychology of a drug habit does not encourage moderation or rational behavior. Thus, drug abuse is a general social problem as well as an individual psychological problem.

The Impact of Drug Use on the Individual

Damage to the individual user from excessive drug use is largely psychological and sociological. This has a marked affect upon the social structure of a community. A person addicted to or dependent upon narcotics is unlikely to destroy himself physically, but it is unusual if he is fully assimilated into the mainstream of the community. Addicts are described as being

[6]Alamo Area Council of Government Report. "Student Drug Survey." LEAA Grant, San Antonio, Texas, May, 1970. The views of at least 20 experts are expressed.

[7]The Interagency Council on Drug Abuse, *Task Force Reports* (Austin, Texas: Texas Criminal Justice Council, 1970) p. A–10.

inadequate, immature, passive, and dependent.[8] Thus, the problem of rehabilitation becomes a monumental task. Drug abusers alienate themselves from society because:

1. In order to "connect" for his drug, the user becomes part of the twilight segment of society that must steal, pander, or turn to prostitution in order to maintain a habit.
2. Drug abuse causes the user to lose contact with the "square" world since his social contacts become more directed toward other users.
3. Drugs attract adolescents, the frustrated, and the culturally handicapped. Thus, youth and minority groups are natural victims.
4. Drug sales support other users, who in turn support the professional, a non-user who is likely to be affiliated with organized criminal groups.

The problems and dangers associated with the heavy use of narcotics such as opiates are easily recognized by the public. The plight of a narcotic addict is somewhat similar to that of an alcoholic a number of years ago. The community today may be lenient to a degree with the alcoholic, but not so with a narcotic addict. The addict is immediately forced into a situation where his constant and immediate concern pertains to obtaining money for the purpose of supporting the increasing cost of his narcotic habit. The public does not fully understand the isolation that surrounds nearly all excessive drug users.

Where there is a liberal attitude toward the use of drugs such as marihuana, the police officer is caught in the dilemma of having to justify his enforcement actions because marihuana does no apparent physical damage. But the same argument could be used for heroin or any other illegal activity. Until research is completed on the biological effects of certain drugs and until state legislatures decide which drugs should be legal, the law enforcement officer is committed to support the existing law.[9]

Dr. Edward R. Bloomquist recognized the dangers of drug abuse as early as 1962.

"We have an almost unlimited supply of drugs which can alter man's perceptivity and behavioral patterns. Some do so with a

___

[8] Daniel Glaser and Vincent Oleary, *The Control and Treatment of Narcotic Use* (Washington, D.C.: Government Printing Office, 1969) p. 15.

[9] See Appendix for state laws governing drug usage penalties.

An Overview of the Drug Abuse Problem

few adverse affects and are thus useful drugs. Others are so unpredictable that their adverse reactions outweigh their beneficial effects. Marihuana is an example of such a detrimental drug."[10]

In the same presentation Dr. Bloomquist compared marihuana to cigarettes and to alcohol, and although he did not minimize these dangers, he pointed out that each use of marihuana gives the user "multiple doses" and the user cannot predict his reaction. Further research has not refuted these observations.

There are many and varied effects of marihuana. The use of this drug creates readily identifiable physiological changes. Marihuana intoxication causes an abnormal lowering of body temperature, a low concentration of sugar in the blood, and a loss of motor coordination. Marihuana also has a severe impact on the nervous system and can produce all the hallucinogenic effects experienced under the influence of LSD.

Several experts concur that marihuana is a dangerous and unstable drug. Its use leads to unpredictable behavior that often results in criminal actions. Marihuana should not be categorized as an innocuous drug. Its use can lead to psychoses lasting from a few hours to many days. Continued use may cause disruption of thought processes, speech disturbances, hallucinations, loss of memory, and other undesirable side-effects. In spite of these opinions, no empirical data has been produced that identify the effects of marihuana.

Studies have been presented to indicate that drugs of the opiate classifications, glues, solvents, and certain hallucinogens all present known dangers. It is the borderline drugs such as marihuana that the public questions. Although there is public disagreement concerning most drugs, law officers must enforce existing laws.

A pioneer in drug research, Dr. Sidney Cohn of U.C.L.A. and formerly of the Narcotics and Drugs Abuse Division of the National Institute of Mental Health, has pointed out in several statements that the use of LSD has tapered off while heroin is now common among high school and college students. He believes the quality of life experienced by a young person is the only hope for curbing drug abuse. It is easy to conclude that education and prevention offer a better chance for drug control than programs of a punitive nature.

[10] Edward R. Bloomquist, *Marihuana: Social Benefit or Social Detriment* (Speech presented at Los Angeles State College, 1962).

Expert Opinions on Drug Abuse in Society

If a state has the right to regulate the private affairs of an individual for the benefit of others, then the necessity for the stringent regulation of many drugs is clear. This regulation must not only involve punitive isolation but should also be dependent upon a number of community resources and coordinated efforts. Communities contain many resources that can be coordinated in order to develop a maximum thrust toward accomplishing voluntary regulation of drug use. These resources could include representatives of major industrial complexes, community businessmen, women's leagues, physicians, and spokesmen for the criminal justice system as well as law enforcement officers.

An Overview of the Drug Abuse Problem

Identifying the Common Drugs

Before an officer is able to take enforcement action he should be able to recognize many of the illegal drugs. Some of the more common drugs will have an identifiable appearance while others will be in a form that may require sophisticated analysis for identification. For purposes of general classification the following figures illustrate some of the more common drugs coming to the attention of law enforcement agencies. Because of the complexity of the drug classifications, the officer should use the tables for reference during his reading and not attempt to memorize the contents of the tables.

To assist the field officer in identifying drug names and types these drug classifications are illustrated:

1. A legal drug classification used in field identification
2. The physiological and psychological classification
3. Recognition and identification of the common dangerous and exotic drugs

Common Legal Drug Classifications

The commonly recognized basis for drug prosecution is the legal classification of the drug under federal, state, or local law. The drug classifications in Figure 2.1, while not meeting the standards for all federal or state laws, present a general discussion of the various drugs encountered by the field officer.

In many states, the most frequent patterns of law identify narcotics violations as felonies while the non-narcotic dangerous drugs and some exotics are classified as misdemeanors. There seems to be little agreement among state statutes regarding the

chapter

2

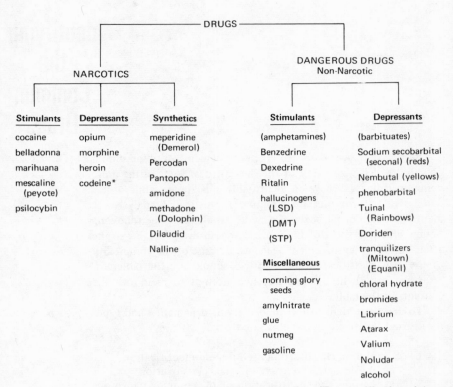

Figure 2.1. Common legal drug classifications. (The classification of drugs may vary from state to state. All are not necessarily prohibited by law; i.e., glue, alcohol, etc. Under the Drug Abuse Control Act illegal delivery, unauthorized possession except by ultimate consumer, a person over 18 giving or selling to anyone under 21, or the filling by a pharmacist of a prescription more than 5 times, or of one older than 6 months, all are acts constituting a federal felony.)

penalty for many of the synthetics or special drugs such as LSD, DMT, and STP. Some confusion has been eliminated by the adoption of the Drug Abuse Control Amendments of 1965, cited in Appendix 2, which make some violations involving dangerous and hallucinogenic drugs federal felonies.

Most states have adopted the Uniform Narcotic Drug Act in some modified version for the control of "hard narcotics." These statutes prohibit the use and sale of habit-forming narcotic drugs, sale and possession of hypnotic drugs, and provide for the confinement or regulation of drug addicts. Habitual users and persons under the influence of drugs are prohibited from driving on the highways. Table Two lists such dependence-producing drugs.

Identifying the Common Drugs

Systemic Analgesics

Natural Opiates
  opium
  morphine
  heroin
  codeine
  Pantopon
  Dilaudid
  Numorphan
Synthetic Opiates
  Dolophine (methadone)

Demerol (meperidine)
Leritine (anileridine)
Narcotic Antagonists
  Nalline (nalorphine)
  cyclazocine
Nonnarcotic Analgesics
  aspirin
  phenacetin
  acetanilid
  Darvon

Central Nervous System Depressants

Barbiturates
  Luminal (phenobarbital)
  Nembutal (pentobarbital)
  Seconal (secobarbital)
  Amytal (amobarbital)
  Tuinal (secobarbital and
    amobarbital)

Nonbarbiturate Sedatives
  Miltown (meprobamate)
  Equanil (meprobamate)
  Doriden
  Placidyl
  paraldehyde
  chloral hydrate
Alcohol

Central Nervous System Stimulants

Amphetamines
  Benzedrine (amphetamine)
  Biphetamine (amphetamine)
  Desoxyn (methamphetamine)
  Dexedrine (dextroamphetamine)

Dexamyl (dextroamphetamine
  and amobarbital)
Cocaine
Caffeine
Nicotine

Psychotropics

Tranquilizers
1. Major
  Phenothiazines
    Thorazine (chlorpromazine)
    Sparine
    Compazine
    Stelazine
    Mellaril
  Reserpates
    Serpasil (reserpine)
    Harmonyl
2. Minor
  Atarax
  Librium
  Valium

Antidepressants
  Marplan
  Nardil
  Parnate
  Tofranil
  Elavil
Hallucinogens
  LSD
  psilocybin
  mescaline (peyote)
  DMT
Marihuana

Extracted from Richard Brotman and Alfred Freedman, "A Community Mental Health Approach to Drug Addiction" (Washington, D.C.: Government Printing Office, 1968), p. 43.

*The drugs listed all affect the central nervous system in some way; major divisions are made by the primary characteristics of that effect. Brand names are capitalized. When the generic name is in common use, it is given without capitalization. This list is by no means complete (for example, mace, bay leaves, glue, gasoline, cleaning fluid, antihistamines, and morning glory seeds are not included). However, it does include those substances which have received most attention by legal and medical authorities.

In the final analysis, controlled distribution of any drug must originate with the federal government and drug manufacturers. In accordance with new federal legislation, commercial firms must now maintain more rigid inventory controls.

Preliminary Identification of certain

For use by
law enforcement
agencies

RESTRICTED DRUGS

Federal law prohibits sale of AMPHETAMINES and BARBITURATES without a doctor's prescription, or refilling of a prescription without consent of the doctor.

BARBITURATES are sedatives. They affect people much like alcohol. Overconsumption may cause death. Suspect them as possible cause in connection with: delinquency, intoxication, coma, accidents, death.

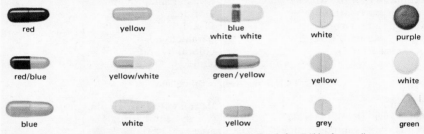

Typical Barbiturate Drugs.*   Also known as "red birds," "goof balls," "yellow jackets," "blue heavens," etc.

AMPHETAMINES are stimulants. When improperly used they tend to create reckless behavior. May be a cause in connection with accidents, wild parties, assaults, delinquency, and burglary.

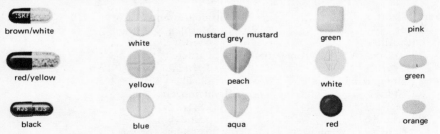

Typical Amphetamine Drugs* ("bennies").   Also known as pep pills, co-pilots, hearts, footballs, etc.

*Both barbiturates and amphetamines come in a wide variety of sizes, shapes, and colors.   These are only a few typical examples.   In any case, positive identification should be made by chemical test.   Write the Food and Drug Administration office listed below for information about these tests.

These drugs are **_not_** narcotics, but watch out for them.   If illegal sale is suspected, please notify:

Figure 2.2.   A reproduction of an identification sheet supplied to local officers by the federal law enforcement agencies.

Identifying the Common Drugs

BARBITURATE IDENTIFIER

HOW TO USE IDENTI-CODE

A special letter-number symbol appears on each Lilly capsule and tablet and on each label of suppositories and powders for oral suspension. By checking this code against the *Identi-Code Index*, you will be able to identify each unit quickly and accurately.

red   blue

"F" = Pulvule®   "64" = TUINAL®
SODIUM AMOBARBITAL AND
SODIUM SECOBARBITAL

The letter in the Identi-Code shows the Lilly product form; the number indicates the specific product name and its formula. In this case, "F64" identifies the Pulvule as Tuinal. Reference to the *Identi-Code Index* shows that Tuinal (F64) contains 25 mg. sodium amobarbital and 25 mg. sodium secobarbital.

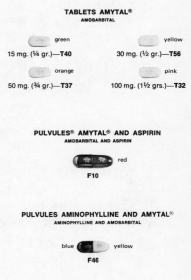

TABLETS AMYTAL®
AMOBARBITAL

green
15 mg. (¼ gr.)—**T40**

yellow
30 mg. (½ gr.)—**T56**

orange
50 mg. (¾ gr.)—**T37**

pink
100 mg. (1½ grs.)—**T32**

PULVULES® AMYTAL® AND ASPIRIN
AMOBARBITAL AND ASPIRIN

red
F10

PULVULES AMINOPHYLLINE AND AMYTAL®
AMINOPHYLLINE AND AMOBARBITAL

blue   yellow
F46

Furnished courtesy of the Eli Lilly Company

Figure 2.3. How drug manufacturers are attempting to identify and control inventory.

Recognizing Some of the Common Dangerous and Exotic Drugs

The preliminary identification of certain drugs is important for the field officer. These drugs may commonly be found at the scene of accidents or parties, and may be encountered in investigations unrelated to drugs. The government publication cited in Figure 2.2 makes it possible to identify and compare some of the common brands.

Figure 2.3 is an example of how one manufacturer identifies its product. Generic names will frequently be difficult to identify unless the name of the manufacturer is known.

Exotic Drugs

This classification includes several drugs, often referred to as exotic drugs, which are hallucinogens or psychedelics. Research

Exotic Drugs

17

and field observation indicate that these drugs produce sensations such as distortions of space, sound, color and other effects. The possession of some of these drugs is a felony under the Drug Abuse Control Act. The groups include:

Lysergic acid derivatives—*LSD*
Phenylethylamine derivatives—*mescaline, peyote*
Tryptamine derivatives—*psilocybin* (from the mushroom *Psilocybe mexicana*)
Piperidyl benzylate esters—*Ditran*
Phencyclidine or Sernyl
Amphetamine derivatives—*MDA, MMDA*, and *dimethoxymethyl amphetamine (STP)*
Miscellaneous—*ololiqui (morning glory), nutmeg, muscarine* (from the *Amanita* mushrooms), *jimson weed (atropine and scopolamine)*

In addition to the chemical composition of various drug types, the field officer should be aware of drug classes from the psychopharmacological viewpoint cited in Table Three.

Identifying the Common Drugs

Drug Class	Group	Example	Common Name
PSYCHOTHERAPEUTICS—used in the treatment of psychological and psychiatric disorders			
ANTI-PSYCHOTICS—used primarily to treat major psychoses	ANTI-PSYCHOTIC: *Rauwolfia* alkaloids phenothiazines	reserpine chloropromazine	Serpasil Thorazine
ANTI-ANXIETY drugs—used to treat neurotic conditions, and reduce psychological stress	ANTI-ANXIETY: propanediols benzodiazepines barbiturates	meprobamate chlordiazepoxide phenobarbital	Miltown Librium see SEDATIVES
ANTI-DEPRESSANTS—used in the treatment of psychiatric depression	ANTI-DEPRESSANT: MAO* inhibitors dibenzazepines	tranylcypromine imipramine	Parnate Tofranil
PSYCHOTOMIMETICS—produce changes in mood, thinking, and behavior	Ergot derivatives *Cannabis sativa* *Lophophora williamsii* *Psilocybe mexicana*	lysergic acid diethylamide marihuana mescaline psilocybin	Lysergide, LSD hemp, hashish peyote button

*MAO abbreviation for monoamine oxidase (an enzyme)

Exotic Drugs

Drug Class	Group	Example	Common Name
STIMULANTS—elevate mood, increase confidence and alertness, and prevent fatigue	Sympathomimetics	amphetamine	Benzedrine
	analeptics	pentylenetetrazol	Metrazol
	psychotomimetics	lysergic acid diethylamide	Lysergide, LSD
	nicotinics	nicotine	
	xanthines	caffeine	
SEDATIVES AND HYPNOTICS—used to treat mental stress, insomnia, and anxiety	bromides	potassium bromide	
	barbiturates	phenobarbital	Luminal
	chloral derivatives	chloral hydrate	
	alcohols	ethanol	
ANESTHETICS, ANALGESICS, AND PARALYTICS—widely used in the field of medicine			
GENERAL ANESTHETICS act centrally to cause a loss of consciousness.	general anesthetics	nitrous oxide	"laughing gas"
		diethyl ether	
		chloroform	
LOCAL ANESTHETICS act only at or near the site of application.	local anesthetics	cocaine	coca
		procaine	
ANALGESIC drugs produce euphoria and stupor, and are effective pain relievers.	analgesics	opium derivatives	morphine, heroin
PARALYTIC drugs produce motor (muscular) paralysis.	paralytics	tubocurarine	curare

†Table 1 is extracted from Brotman and Freedman, op. cit., pp. 44-50.

Identifying the Common Drugs

Common Drugs: A Brief History and Description

Each type of drug has had its unique impact upon society. The characteristics of a drug will frequently dictate the type and location of enforcement necessary to control its distribution and use. Table Four provides only brief information for a select group of drugs constituting the major drug enforcement problem. In this group, based only on an unscientific legal classification, are (1) narcotics, (2) non-narcotics or dangerous drugs, and (3) hallucinogenics.

Narcotics

Narcotics are referred to as stimulants and depressants, depending on their physiological effects.

Stimulants

Cocaine is one of the more powerful stimulants. It comes from the mountainous regions of South America where the cocoa leaf is grown. These leaves are processed into cocaine and smuggled into the United States through Miami, New York, and other major international ports of entry.[1]

Cocaine is not in popular demand because of its price (four to five times as expensive as heroin). It is used primarily for "stabilizing" the central nervous system when heroin is being used.

Cocaine users report they have elations, hallucinations, and the sensation of foreign objects under the skin. This is caused by

[1] Federal Bureau of Narcotics and Drug Abuse, *Fact Sheet No. 3* (Washington, D.C.: Government Printing Office, 1969) p. 3-1.

chapter

3

Table Four

Drug Classification and Common Testing Procedures

Drug	Source	Identification	Chemical Tests
MARIHUANA	*Cannabis sativa* Annual plant Herbaceous 2–8 feet high Dioecious Female plant produces greater active principle	Stems upright rectilinear fluted Branches short fragile Leaves palmate compound—5 to 11 lacerated serrated pinnately veined	Stem contains calcium carbonate; hydrochloric acid will release carbon dioxide bubbles. *Duquenois (modified)*
OPIUM	Opium poppy *Papaver somniferum* juice of unripe pods	Dark tan to black Solid to liquid Tar appearing	Burning—sweet smell Marquis Wagners Meyers
CODEINE (methylmorphine)	Opium Synthetic	White crystalline Powder, Tablets	Marquis Wagners Mechkes Olivers
MORPHINE	Opium Synthetic	Powder tablets Capsules, cubes Solids—white to yellow Solutions—colorless	Marquis Wagners Mechkes Olivers
HEROIN (Diacetylmorphine)	Opium Synthetic	powder, capsules White to gray—tan	Marquis Wagners Mechkes Olivers

Drug	Source	Identification	Chemical Tests
Dilaudid (dihydromorphine)	Opium Synthetic	White powder, tablets	Wagners Marquis Mechkes Olivers
Paregoric	Opium	Opium solution in alcohol with camphor	Wagners Dehydrate-burn Marquis Mechkes
Laudanum	Opium	Tincture of opium (solution in alcohol)	Wagners Dehydrate-burn Marquis Mechkes
Isonipecaine (meperidine hydrochloride) TRADE NAMES Demerol Dolantin Endolat Pethidone	Synthetic	White tablets	Wagners X-ray diffraction Infrared spectrum Gold chloride
Methadone hydrochloride TRADE NAMES Methadon Amidone Amidon Dolophine Adanon	Synthetic	White powder Liquid A	Wagners X-ray diffraction Infrared spectrum Picric acid

Table Four (cont.)

Drug	Source	Identification	Chemical Tests
Cocaine (methylbenzoylecgonine)	Coco leaves Synthetic	White crystalline powder "Snow"	Wagners Melting point Cobalt thiocyanate Gold chloride
Amphetamines Dextroamphetamine Dexedrine, Benzedrine Desoxyephedrine Methamphetamine	Synthetic	Solutions, powder Tablets, capsules	Ultraviolet X-ray diffraction and Infrared spectra Color test Odor test
Barbiturates	Synthetic	Solutions, powder Tablets, capsules Seconal—red capsule Nembutal—yellow Tuinal—red and blue Phenobarbital— triangular & round tablets	Koppani X-ray diffraction Infrared Spectrum
Lysergic acid diethylamide	Synthetic	Colorless liquid	Infrared Spectrum
Mescaline trimethoxy-phenylethylamine)	Lophophora williamsii	Appears to be mushrooms, Cluster of button-like growths	Microcrystalline test Gold chloride and phosphoric acid Acetic acid and platinium chloride Chromatographic analysis Infrared spectrum

the desensitization of sensory nerve endings. Many users reported excruciating pain when a bed sheet was placed on them. Cocaine is commonly used with heroin to create multiple sensations giving the elation of cocaine and the longer effect of heroin. This mixture of heroin and cocaine is called a "speedball." Cocaine is frequently "horned" by inhalation and absorption through the membranes of the nose or mouth. Cocaine resembles fluffy sugar crystals and is referred to as "snow" as shown in Figure 3.1.

Marihuana (*Cannabis sativa*) is a stimulant popularly known as "pot," "tea," "weed," "grass," or "Mary Jane." The social attitudes held by the public about this drug are quite different from those held about opium, heroin, and other "hard" drugs. The investigator does not find ready public assistance in marihuana investigations. Marihuana seems to be morally acceptable since the physiological effects of smoking marihuana have not been empirically documented. Some evidence however, suggests that there may be psychological damage due to prolonged marihuana use.

Marihuana is used in various forms and different ways throughout the world. It may be used by smoking in a cigarette or an oriental water pipe; or powdering the leaves, then mixing honey and spices to be eaten, drunk like a milkshake, or smoked. Hashish is made from the resin of the flowering tops of the plant and kneaded into sticks or soles or reduced to powder form.

Historically, marihuana may be traced to almost all parts of the world. The uses of marihuana in most countries are primarily socially or religiously oriented. In the United States marihuana has been popularized in usage by the Southwestern Indians. There are, however, references to its use at Jamestown, Virginia, and other early colonies. Incidents in the Civil War cite marihuana usage.

Much of the marihuana coming into the United States is smuggled from Mexico. Since 1967, there have been indications that tons of the drug have been shipped from Cuba via Canada and Mexico.

The marihuana plant may be identified in this manner:

1. It has the appearance of a poinsettia plant.
2. It has narrow serrated leaves formed in an uneven number, such as five, seven, or nine.
3. The top of the leaf is a bright, dark green. The underside is a duller, lighter green.
4. The underside of the leaf has hairlike protrusions.

Narcotics

MARIHUANA
STIMULANT
INDIAN HEMP · HASHISH · BHANG

TOP SIDE — BRIGHT GREEN

BOTTOM OF LEAF — HAIR-LIKE APPEARANCE

RESIN FROM FLOWERING
TOPS OF PLANT KNEADED
INTO STICKS OR POWDER

CANNABIS SATIVA

HALF CAN — MANICURED

MARIHUANA CIGARETTES
ARE ALWAYS WRAPPED
IN TWO WRAPPERS

ROACH
AND
DEBRIS

COCAINE
STIMULANT

BITTER ALKALOID — $C_{17}H_{21}NO_4$

"COKE"

COCAINE CRYSTALS

HABITUAL USE — "COCAINISM"

(OBTAINED FROM COCOA LEAVES)

THE MIRROR OF YOUR SOUL

NORMAL　　　　CONTRACTED　　　　DILATED　　　　THE USER SEES US

Figure 3.1.   Common stimulant narcotics.

5. The dried flowers and leaves of the plant are "manicured" and generally smoked as a cigarette.
6. The quality of marihuana will vary with the maturity of the plant, the position on the plant from which the material is taken, the location of harvest, and how well the leaves have been cured.

Marihuana is further identified by description and by method of processing (see Figure 3.2).

1. Processing is done by rubbing marihuana between the hands then separating the seeds and stems from the leafy material.
2. Unlike cured tobacco, marihuana will always remain green. Processing will cause the leaf to be broken into small pieces.
3. The marihuana cigarette will usually be wrapped in two thicknesses of cigarette paper.
4. The cigarette will be smaller in diameter and shorter than a regular cigarette and tucked in at both ends.
5. It will smell similar to dried grass or alfalfa and will contain seeds and debris along with leafy material.

Figure 3.2. Marihuana being rolled into cigarettes—note that two thicknesses of paper are used.

Narcotics

27

The enforcement of marihuana laws depends primarily upon information supplied by informers, police operators, or investigations of other crimes. Marihuana may be visually identified when it is being smoked or it may be identified from its distinctive sweet, musty smell. When smoking a marihuana cigarette, the user may cup his hands over the cigarette and his nostrils, then inhale the smoke in quick, deep puffs. These deep puffs will cause the cigarette to glow brightly in the dark and may assist in establishing probable cause for an arrest. Marihuana usage may be recognized from ordinary activity if the person appears to be intoxicated, if the eyes are bloodshot and dilated, and if the pupils will not react to light.

> In a social setting marihuana tends to create:
> sociability
> hilarity
> pleasure in sight, sound and other senses
> harmonious relationships
> In an isolated setting it:
> tranquilizes
> relaxes
> encourages contemplation
> In a tense situation it causes a user to:
> act irrationally
> react quickly
> become disoriented in logical decision-making.
> (Experts disagree about the role of marihuana as a violence motivator. While it may not create violence, it tempers the nervous system to react in a way as to induce violent reactions in stress situations.)

Other stimulant narcotics frequently encountered by local law enforcement officers are peyote, mescaline, and psilocybin. Belladonna, a derivative of the nightshade mushroom of South America, is rarely encountered.

Peyote. History traces peyote to the mountains of northern Mexico. It was used by the Chicimea tribe before the Christian era, and Indian legends attribute a divine origin to peyote. During the seventeenth century a peyote cult used the drug for medicinal and hallucinatory purposes. In the nineteenth century the Mescalero-Apaches of New Mexico, as well as the Comanches, the Kiowas, and other tribes, became users of the drug. Today the drug is legal when used by the Native American Church in their religious ceremonies.

Common Drugs: A Brief History and Description

Mescaline. The active substance of the peyote cactus, phenyl-ethylamine, causes much the same reaction as marihuana. The hallucinations, however, may be seen in color. Mescaline comes in "cactus buttons" or as a powder. The buttons may easily be mistaken for mushrooms. Peyote is illustrated in Figure 3.3.

Psilocybin. This drug is isolated from the *Psilocybe* mushroom. Psilocylin gives substantially the same reaction as marihuana except the hallucinations may be in color, creating a psychological rather than a physical dependence.

Depressants

Depressant narcotics of the most common variety are derivatives of the opium poppy.

Opium. This depressant narcotic is the source for other drugs such as morphine, heroin, codeine, and pantopon. Raw opium is produced in the Middle East, the Orient, and Mexico. Through

Figure 3.3 The peyote cactus.

Narcotics

organized groups, raw opium is moved to processing plants where it is reduced to the desired product.

Opium has a history of ten thousand years or more. It was used by the early Romans and Greeks, and has been influential in Chinese history in the opium wars of the 1840s and 1850s. It was used by the Japanese to control mass populations during their occupation of China during the 1930s. Opium producing countries today are said to be Turkey, India, China, Mexico, and some countries in Southeast Asia.

Opium is usually smoked, although it may be taken in other ways. Opium of smoking quality is called "mud," "hop," "tar," or "Ah Pen Yen." The opium is rolled into balls about the size of a large pea which may be heated and smoked. It is sometimes eaten and opium in this form is referred to as "Yen Pocks" or "Pills." Opium is shown in Figure 3.4.

The reduction of opium to heroin is a complex process that requires extensive laboratory equipment. Sulphuric acid is one of the main ingredients which gives heroin its bitter taste. This process is shown in Figure 3.5.

Morphine. Morphine is a depressant narcotic and is a primary derivative of opium. This drug was developed in Germany in 1805 as a cure for opium addicts. It was first thought to be non-addicting, but in reality, it is far more addicting than opium.

Morphine acts as a cerebral depressant and a spinal stimulant. It is commonly given orally or intravenously to control severe pain. Morphine is used principally by:

1. Older addicts; it has a physical holding power but does not produce the flash commonly felt from heroin use.
2. Persons who can go to a doctor who will prescribe it as a medicine.
3. Persons who buy it through either legal or illegal prescriptions.

Heroin. Heroin was developed in 1898 in Germany also as a cure for opium addiction. However, the end result has been that heroin is one of the most powerfully addicting drugs available. It is said to be at least twenty times stronger than opium and ten times more addicting than morphine.

Heroin has been used extensively throughout the United States since 1945. It accounts for 90 percent of the felony narcotic arrests and could easily be classified as the leading problem drug. Heroin is described as being very light in consistency, having

Common Drugs: A Brief History and Description

OPIUM
DEPRESSANT

POPPY BOLLS—GUM OPIUM — 3000 TONS ANNUALLY
SOFT, RUBBERY, LIGHT IN COLOR

TINCTURE OF OPIUM—GRANULATED OR POWDERED (PARAGORIC)
FOUR PERCENT TINCTURE OF OPIUM

SMOKING OPIUM—HOP TOY (BINDLE)

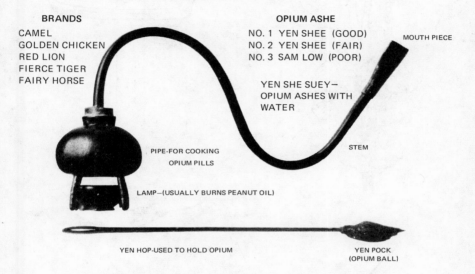

BRANDS	OPIUM ASHE
CAMEL	NO. 1 YEN SHEE (GOOD)
GOLDEN CHICKEN	NO. 2 YEN SHEE (FAIR)
RED LION	NO. 3 SAM LOW (POOR)
FIERCE TIGER	
FAIRY HORSE	YEN SHE SUEY— OPIUM ASHES WITH WATER

MOUTH PIECE

PIPE-FOR COOKING
OPIUM PILLS

STEM

LAMP—(USUALLY BURNS PEANUT OIL)

YEN HOP-USED TO HOLD OPIUM

YEN POCK
(OPIUM BALL)

YEN GOW— USED TO SCRAPE INSIDE OF PIPE BOWL

YUCK YEN— ONE PART SMOKING OPIUM TO SEVEN PARTS
MING YING (CHINESE HERB)

2½ TAEL CAN	3⅓ OZ. – SIZE OF HALF TOBACCO CAN
5 TAEL CAN	7 OZ. – SIZE OF ONE TOBACCO CAN

MORPHINE
DEPRESSANT

$C_{17} H_{19} NO_3 H_2O$ – 1805, GERMANY – MOST IMPORTANT

NARCOTIC PRINCIPLE OF OPIUM – REFINED INTO HEROIN
MORPHINE SULPHATE' DIONIN DILAUDID AND APOMORPHINE –CODEINE–PAPERVINE

Figure 3.4. Opium with brand names and the primary derivative, morphine.

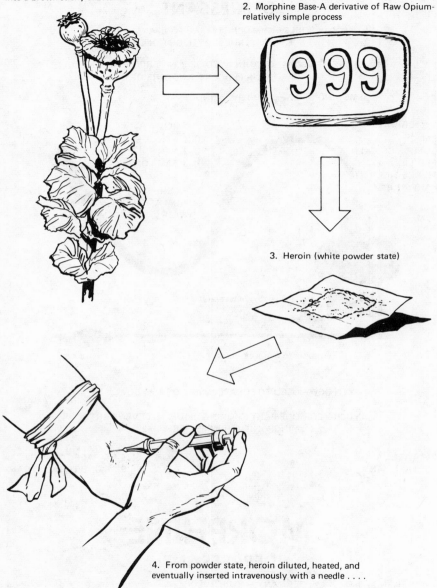

1. Raw opium is scraped from the seed pod of the poppy plant. First, incisions are made in the pod to let the milky opium fluid drain and dry overnight into a brown sticky substance

2. Morphine Base-A derivative of Raw Opium-relatively simple process

3. Heroin (white powder state)

4. From powder state, heroin diluted, heated, and eventually inserted intravenously with a needle . . . .

Figure 3.5 . The conversion of opium to heroin.

Common Drugs: A Brief History and Description

the appearance of talcum powder. It is light in weight, a cigarette package when full would weigh less than one ounce. Pure processed heroin is white; some Mexican heroin, due to poor processing methods, is a light brown. Heroin has an acidic smell and a bitter taste. Figure 3.6 shows heroin being "capped up."

Heroin finds little popular support even among the heavy narcotic users. Heroin has no redeeming medicinal value and is referred to as the monster of all drugs. (See Figure 3.7.)

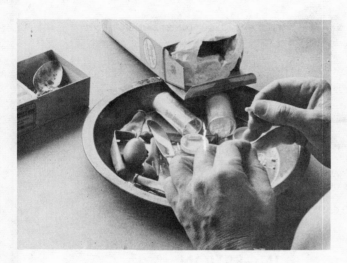

Figure 3.6. The heroin peddler "capping up." This is a slow process, and the street peddler can easily be seized when engaged in this activity.

Narcotics

HEROIN
DEPRESSANT

$C_{21} H_{33} NO_5$ — DERIVATIVE OF MORPHINE — GERMANY — 1898
20 TIMES STRONGER THAN OPIUM — 10 TIMES MORE ADDICTIVE THAN MORPHINE

TOOLS OF THE TRADE

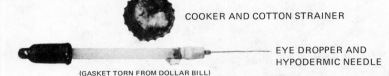

COOKER AND COTTON STRAINER

EYE DROPPER AND
HYPODERMIC NEEDLE

(GASKET TORN FROM DOLLAR BILL)

A SHARP NAIL IS COMMONLY USED TO OPEN
THE VEIN FOR INJECTION WITH EYE DROPPER

INJECTION

COOK UP "H" IN WATER — SOLUTION INJECTED BY NEEDLE
— INTO SKIN — "SKIN POP"
— INTO VEIN — "MAIN LINE" FULL EFFECT IN ONE
OR TWO MINUTES

INGESTION

RAW HEROIN IS "HORNED" INTO THE NOSE
HEROIN ERODES NASAL MEMBRANES
SEPTUM DIVIDING NOSTRILS IS EATEN AWAY

(USED I/D BY NALLINE TEST)

METHODS OF PACKAGING

HEROIN CAPSULES
BROWN CAPS
ARE FROM MEXICO
(NOT REFINED)

TWO GRAMS
OF
HEROIN CAPS

TOP BALLOON
"H" IS DOUBLE
WRAPPED FOR
CARRYING IN MOUTH

MIDDLE BALLOON
CONTAINS HEROIN
CAPS—ONE GRAM

BOTTOM BALLOON
CONTAINS BULK
HEROIN — ONE HALF
SPOONFUL

Figure 3.7. Heroin and implements of the trade.

Codeine. This drug is used in cough medicine in diluted quantities or in tablet form. It is used by the street addict primarily when no stronger drug is available. In quantity codeine can sustain a heroin addict's physical needs until he can acquire more heroin.

The international sources of opiates are said to be the Far East, Southern France, and Mexico. Despite a concentrated effort by many governments, most opium derivatives will probably originate from these sources in the foreseeable future.

Dangerous Drugs

For every person involved in hard narcotics there are thousands using and abusing the non-narcotic or dangerous drugs. These drugs are of such a wide variety that only a few of the more common types are mentioned here. The major categories are: (1) stimulants, (2) depressants, and (3) hallucinogenics.

Stimulants

Amphetamines are the most widely used dangerous drugs that involve the police. These drugs are dangerous primarily because of the unpredictable reactions they induce in the user. Excessive users of stimulant drugs become exceedingly dangerous when driving or when they become involved in a criminal activity. Persons using stimulants may exhibit these traits:

1. Eyes will be dilated; the user often wears dark glasses to reduce the glare of light and minimize the dilation of the pupils.
2. Nervous energy; the heat user cannot sit still, many will scratch sores on their arms, legs, neck, etc.
3. Erratic movements; the user will step high when stepping upon a curb, over an object, or up steps.
4. Violent response to stress situations; in many instances creating problems that may lead to questioning and arrest.
5. Confused thinking; a user may become disoriented when answering questions.
6. The heavy user will hallucinate and suffer psychological withdrawals.

For generic names and common tests of identification, refer to Table Four. There are hundreds of trade names and varieties for pills and capsules. The most common ones are cited in Figures 4 and 5, Chapter 11.

Caution should be exercised in the investigation and arrest of all persons possessing dangerous drugs since many drugs may be legally obtained on prescription. While the law explicitly directs that the prescription must be with the drug, this does not always happen. The officer should attempt to determine if the drugs in question are actually issued to the possessor by a legal prescription and attempt to locate the source of supply if illegality is suspected.

The more common types of stimulants are:

Amphetamine sulfate, benzedrine or "bennies." Benzedrine affects the body in these ways:
Creates a feeling of excess energy
May give one a feeling of hostility toward another person
Makes one highly nervous and agitated
Excessive use will cause hallucinations
Can cause paranoia and eventually psychosis
Dextro-amphetamine sulfate, dexedrine or "dexies." The body's reaction to this drug is substantially the same as to benzedrine.
Methamphetamine hydrochloride, Methedrine or "speed" is often called the worst of the stimulating drugs. The longtime abuser will:
Have paranoidal hallucinations
Suffer impairment of mental functions
Lose emotional control
The typical user of "speed" is socially shunned because of the obnoxious attitudes generated by the drug. The withdrawal symptoms are compared to heroin.

Unlike the opiate drugs, amphetamines do not produce physical dependence or withdrawal illness, but prolonged use leads to a severe state of nervousness and often causes emotional dependence.[2]

Depressants

The barbiturates are potent drugs frequently encountered in police investigations. The most common varieties encountered are the sleeping pills which are legally acquired under prescription.

[2]Glaser and Oleary, *op. cit.*

Common Drugs: A Brief History and Description

Most users could secure these drugs legally, however the increased cost of a prescription and medical fees makes it more desirable to obtain them on the illegal market.

The primary police concerns in dealing with barbiturates are to keep users from driving motor vehicles and to protect the user from himself. For example, these drugs used in combination with alcohol frequently have a "compounding effect" that causes many accidental overdoses which often result in death. Persons using these drugs may exhibit these traits:

The heavy user appears to be a sleepy drunk.

He may be in a stupor and while in this condition will be inclined to take more pills, contributing to an overdose and possible death.

The most common drugs in this category are:

Sodium secobarbital, commonly identified by the trade name Seconal and referred to as "reds,"

Sodium pentobarbital, with the trade name Nembutal and referred to as "yellow jackets,"

Phenobarbital, commonly called "pheenies,"

Amobarbital, known by the trade name Amytal and referred to as "blues,"

Secobarbital-amobarbital, with a trade name of Tuinal and referred to as "rainbows" or "double trouble."

The list is endless and the officer will frequently have to use his own good judgment in determining the *prima facie* legality of drugs that come to his attention.

Hallucinogenics

These drugs stimulate the sensory system in such a manner as to produce hallucinations. Psychedelic or mind altering is used in referring to the mental changes encountered. These drugs may affect the body in the following ways:

Sights, sounds and other perceptions are intensified and frequently imaginary ones are created.

The reasoning power of a user may be lost. The loss may be temporary or it may be permanent.

The power to create and think clearly may give way to the wonderful world of euphoria.

Hallucinogenics

Lysergic acid diethylamide or "LSD"

At one time LSD was considered to be the ultimate drug. Those who took the drug described great intellectual and emotional insights. But many reported staggering after-effects.

Under present laws, it is nearly impossible for the police enforcement unit to seize legal evidence of LSD possession. Probable cause supplied by a reliable informant or purchase are about the only two effective methods of enforcement.

In its natural state, LSD is odorless and colorless and is frequently transported in a form that is not easily recognizable. For example, in sugar cubes is popular, or in pale blue liquid or orange powder are common forms. The quality of the product for street trade is often identified by the color.

Because of the highly publicized side-effects, the minute quantity necessary for a dose (about 250 micrograms), and the lasting and recurring hallucinations experienced by the users, many have gone to other drugs such as peyote, DMT, or STP.

Dimethyltryptamine or "DMT"

This drug is a natural product and is also made synthetically. Its effects are similar to LSD but are of shorter duration. Use may be followed by periods of mental disorientation.

Dimethoxymethylamphetamine or "STP"

The common name is taken from serenity, tranquility, peace. It is a synthetic product used to treat mental illnesses, and users have found this drug popular. Its long term effect has been compared with LSD.

Miscellaneous Drugs

Glues and Solvents

In their attempts to escape from reality drug abusers use a variety of substances to achieve intoxication. When an officer encounters a suspect who is "intoxicated" and does not show objective symptoms of alcohol use, he should be taken immediately to a doctor. The doctor may then render an expert opinion as to the degree and cause of the intoxication.

The following discussion identifies some of the common products that may become a subject of police investigation.[3] Laws governing these substances are found in Appendix II.

Glue is compounded from a variety of ingredients; for example, toluol is common base for glue. Airplane glue has trichorethlene. Glue can cause hallucinations resulting in:

euphoria
grandiosity
distortion of space and visual perceptions in vivid colors
muscle tremors

Gasoline, according to unofficial reports, produces psychotic reactions in the human as do LSD, mescaline, morning glory seeds, and nutmeg. Inhalation of the fumes gives feelings of euphoria, recklessness, and some loss of self-control.

Carbon tetrachloride, in addition to making one intoxicated, will produce damage to liver and kidneys. It is a depressant and not frequently used.

The purpose of providing descriptions and a brief review of the common drugs has been to make the field officer aware of a drug's appearance and the cultural setting where it may be used. For example, opium would most likely be found in the asiatic sub-cultures of the major cities. Marihuana and peyote have long histories in the Southwest and thus become somewhat more acceptable to the sub-cultures of that region.

Equipped with a basic knowledge of what he is looking for, the field officer should be better prepared to conduct investigations dealing with drug abuse.

[3]Edward Press, and Alan K. Done, Abstract from *Pediatrics,* 39:541 (1967), and the following edition discussing solvent sniffing: "Physiologic effects and Community control measures for intoxication from the intentional inhalation of organic solvents," Parts I and II.

Miscellaneous Drugs

How to Conduct a Drug Investigation

In addition to the general investigative techniques basic to all crimes there are some techniques which are unique to drug investigations.[1] These include: (1) the use of an informer, (2) techniques in conducting the investigation, and (3) the "buy program" and other miscellaneous investigative techniques.

Use of an Informer

The use of an informer requires caution to insure the personal safety of the informer and to maintain investigative integrity. Since few covert drug investigations could be conducted without an informer's help, there is an obligation on the part of the officer to obtain accurate information without compromising the suspect's legal rights or jeopardizing the integrity of the case through improper use of the informer. An informer may be obtained from a variety of sources:

1. The ranks of drug users.
2. Other criminals such as burglars, petty thieves, and prostitutes.
3. Casual street acquaintances of the field officer.
4. Neighbors and friends of the suspected violators.
5. School personnel, ministers, and businessmen.

The motivation for a person to serve as an informer is not usually known and may influence the credibility of all information received. When an informer gives information, the background of the informer's motives should be questioned:

[1] Refer to Paul B. Weston and Kenneth M. Wells, *Elements of Criminal Investigation* (Englewood Cliffs, New Jersey: Prentice-Hall, Inc., 1970).

chapter

4

1. Does the informer have an ax to grind with the person being informed upon?
2. Does the informer think the person is using drugs because he is strange, dirty, or has friends who are "dopey looking"? Actions rather than looks are generally better indicators of drug usage.
3. Does the informer expect to be allowed to commit crimes and still remain on the street?

An informer, unless his reliability is well established, may try to give information he has heard from a third party or by way of a general rumor. To further verify data, compare the information received against facts that are already known, i.e., names of suspects, descriptions of suspects, house, room, street, etc.

Believe what an informer says only to the extent that all information is recorded and then either verified or discounted. Information one informer cannot give you in complete detail may be supplied by other people.

If an informer is a criminal—and most good ones are—the officer should consider these possibilities:

1. What kind of deal does the informer expect in return for his information?
2. Is the information received going to be worth the price of keeping the informer where he can gain good information? (Is a beat officer going to tolerate a potential criminal on his beat so that information may be secured on the remaining criminals on the street?)
3. Is the information received worth the officer's time?
4. Is the information received from the informer reliable?
5. When does the reliability of the informer have to be established?
6. If the informer does no more than "point an accusing finger" at a suspect, then an "independent investigation" must be conducted. If an officer is able to establish probable cause for an arrest, independent of the original information, the information furnished by the informer is not material. In this event neither the identity nor the reliability of the informer need be brought out in court.
7. Does the officer produce the informer in court? Whenever possible, it is desirable to have the informer as a witness. If there is danger of bodily harm or a possibility that the informer may be used again, then it is not wise to put that informer on the stand. *Never put an informer on the witness stand if prior agreement has been made for him to remain anonymous.*

Use of an Informer

In most states the *privileged communication rule* between officer and informer may be invoked if there is a danger that revealing an informer's identity may *result in death* to the informer.

An officer, regardless of his assignment, should develop a number of informers. In an informer relationship an officer should be explicit about the kind of information he expects. Prior to giving information to an officer, the informer should be instructed to discover the following details about the drug violator being informed upon.

1. A full description of the suspects, with names and aliases.
2. Physical defects such as a limp, hunch back, large nose, etc.
3. What types of clothing does the suspect wear? Color, etc.
4. Does the suspect carry a firearm or knife?
5. Location of residence; does suspect live with relatives?
6. Place where suspect does business, hangouts where he contacts users or suppliers.
7. Location of associates—city, address, etc. (All locations should be given by street number if possible and also verified by cross streets and a physical description of landmarks such as buildings, memorials, or other marks that will tend to verify location.)
8. What are the physical features of the suspect's house or room? Is there a screen door? Do the doors open in or out? What kinds of locks are on the doors and windows? Are there bathroom facilities and where are they located? What are the warning devices such as phones, buzzers, or dogs? Does the suspect leave his room or house on a schedule; does he answer the phone in the hall?
9. Vehicles used by or available to the suspect—including license number, damage spots, and other identifiable marks.
10. Where does suspect carry drugs in his car when traveling?
11. Does the suspect carry a weapon in the vehicle and if so where?
12. Type of drug being sold or used, how is it packaged, and where might it be hidden?
13. When a sale is made does the peddler go into the yard, the garage, or other parts of the house?
14. When a sale is being made and the peddler leaves the room, are any unusual noises made; i.e., opening refrigerator door, going to closet, etc.?
15. Does the peddler carry drugs in his hand, mouth, or on his body?

How to Conduct a Drug Investigation

16. How is the connection made; what time and where does the transaction take place?
17. How can a buyer get introduced or "duked into" a connection?
18. Is there a code word or signal that will get an undercover buyer or raiding officer into the peddler's room or house?
19. Where can surveillance posts be maintained so activity at a suspected place of residence may be observed?
20. Is the room across or down the hall from the suspect vacant?
21. Are neighbors friendly to the suspect?
22. Are there dogs in the room, house, or neighborhood?
23. Are any streets where suspect lives dead-end? Are there trees on the street that may conceal a vehicle at night?

Conducting an Investigation

The field officer will either observe the violation and take immediate action or he will receive information and conduct a preliminary investigation.

Immediate Action by the Officer

The uniformed field officer is in a position to be very effective in street drug enforcement. During his patrol the officer should be alert for:

1. Symptoms of possible drug use such as hypodermic marks, contracted or dilated pupils, sallow complexion, and other objective symptoms that may indicate drug use.
2. Evasive action when an officer approaches; suspect's actions such as dropping or throwing objects or putting objects in his mouth.
3. Suspects hanging around "shooting galleries" such as public restrooms, pool halls, abandoned houses, etc.
4. Evidence of use or sale of drugs during the routine investigation of other crimes.

When immediate action is warranted the officer should not hesitate to take action. A field officer should not normally pass up an arrest in order to give specialized officers time to work on the suspect. *If a violation is observed, take action.* The field officer will usually do preliminary investigations and refer continuing investigations to specialized units. If the circumstances warrant a continuing investigation, an officer's action will be dictated by his department's policies.

Preliminary Investigation

In some instances the preliminary investigation will lead to the clearing of a case either by arrest or other disposition. In the event an immediate arrest is not made the officer should:

1. Attempt to obtain the identity (name, address, etc.) of the informer for a follow-up interview to verify details of information given.
2. Keep a written record in exact detail of *all* information received regarding any drug activity, and forward through channels.
3. Verify as much of the information as possible.
4. Notify concerned agencies if immediate action appears necessary.
   Relay information to the concerned federal agency if interstate or international jurisdiction is evident.
   Establish communications with the Bureau of Narcotics and Dangerous Drugs in the Justice Department for normal interstate operations.
   Inform the Customs Agency Service, Border Patrol, or Treasury Department if international boundries are involved.

Conducting Searches

Cases frequently depend upon the thoroughness of a search. *Prior to any search an informer should be questioned extensively to determine the operating methods of the suspect.* If this is done properly, hours of valuable search time may be saved.

Street peddlers and users are able to carry packets of drugs small enough to hide from normal street frisk. Caution should be exercised in approaching a suspect and surprise is often a valuable technique for approaching a peddler or user. Keep the suspect under continuous observation and always assume that the suspect:

1. May be armed.
2. May be carrying the drug in his hand so that it can be thrown away as the officer approaches.

How to Conduct a Drug Investigation

3. May be carrying the drug in a rubber container in his mouth so that he can swallow it if necessary. *Note:* If the suspect is a heavy user of a depressant drug he may not be able to swallow quickly and will spit out the drug upon demand. If a suspect manages to ingest a quantity of narcotics and there is the possibility of a fatal overdose, the suspect may give permission for a doctor to administer medication which will cause vomiting.

4. May be carrying the drug in a body cavity. If this is known and there is probable cause for an arrest and search, the suspect should be taken to a doctor where the search may be made in a medically approved manner. A body cavity search gives rise to many legal questions and should be conducted in compliance with federal and state law.[2] A search of body cavities should always be made in conjunction with booking procedures and prior to placing a suspected narcotic prisoner in a jail cell.

5. Will in most instances carry the drug in his pocket, hatband, waistband, stocking top, or shoe. He may carry the drug in a cigarette package or in a newspaper or magazine. *Do not allow the suspect to lay a newspaper down and then walk off and "forget" it.* Make sure all papers or magazines are searched prior to being discarded.

6. May tape the drug inside his thighs, under his arm, or in his hair. Do not leave a female without handcuffs, unless there has been a thorough search made, in accordance with departmental policy. During the search keep the suspect isolated from places where drugs might be dropped, such as upholstered furniture, waste baskets, sinks, back seat of patrol car, etc.

The search of a vehicle must be based upon reliable information that drugs are being transported therein. Unless the exact location of a concealment is known, it is often difficult to locate "stash spots." Some of the more common "stash spots" are:

1. A hole in the floor of the vehicle. The drug is placed on the floor near the hole and if the police stop the vehicle, it will be kicked through the hole by the suspect.

2. Gas tanks may be partitioned and entry made through an inspection plate in the trunk floor. The storage part of the partitioned tank may have a cover plate secured with a

[2]Section 242, Title 18 of the U.S. Code has a penalty of one year in prison and a $1,000 fine for depriving a person of his constitutional right to be free of unreasonable searches.

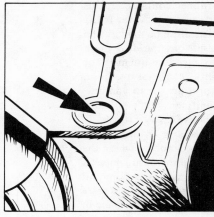

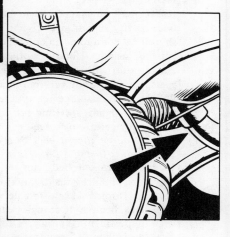

Figure 4.1. Inspection in the trunk of the vehicle may indicate a stash spot in the gas tank.

Figure 4.2. Inspect the rubber air hoses closely. They may slip on and off the heater and air conditioner.

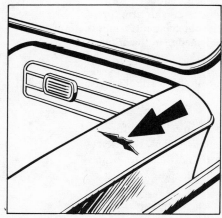

Figure 4.3. Inspect upholstery carefully. This condition observed from outside a Volkswagen revealed ripped upholstery and a stash spot.

Figure 4.4. Air filters, hub caps, and under carriages are common stash spots.

How to Conduct a Drug Investigation

number of metal screws. Unless there is specific information on a vehicle it is unlikely this type of container will
be discovered in a search (see Figure 4.1).

3. Air vents and the surfaces on top of the radio and glove
   compartment are frequently used (see Figure 4.2).

4. Storage space in door panels are accessible when the
   panels can be removed. Torn upholstery, including the
   seats and head liner, offers good concealment (see Figure
   4.3).

5. Undercarriage, compartments welded into frame, hub-
   caps, spare tires, and air filters are popular spots (see
   Figure 4.4).

If a search fails to turn up drugs suspected on the basis of
reliable information, allow the suspect to be left alone in a closed
room (which has just been searched and left clean) for five to ten
minutes. If he is "holding" a drug, it will usually be dumped
under the wastebasket, attached under the edge of table, etc. If
the container he hides is plastic or slick paper, it should then be
tested for fingerprints.

In searching houses and rooms all searches must be based
upon reliable information and a search warrant should be obtained when possible.[3] The location of drugs hidden in a room or
house should be known by the informer and relayed to the
officer prior to the officer's entry. The more common places for
hiding small quantities of drugs may be:

1. Under the sink or washbowl; this usually includes a hypo
   outfit.

2. Taped on top of the door or window, under a drawer,
   chair, or table.

3. Wrapped in a waterproof container and secured inside the
   water storage cabinet of the toilet.

4. Secured with a line and hung out the window. Always
   check before opening the window since the packet of
   drugs will fall to the ground when the window is opened.

5. Inside the light fixture. If a light does not function, check
   inside the socket.

6. Affixed to wood trim and molding, baseboards, under
   stairs, in holes in walls, etc.

[3]Most states have explicit instructions regarding when a search may be
made without a warrant, and provisions allowing an officer to enter a room
without notice to the party therein. Refer also to Chimel vs. California, 89
S.Ct. 2037 (1969) which limits the scope of search in conjunction with a
legal arrest.

Conducting an Investigation

7. In boxes of flour, cereals, or inside a bottle of milk or other liquid.

Miscellaneous Rules Regarding a Search

In order that a case may not be jeopardized, there are rigid rules of search that must be followed. General rules regarding searches are:

1. Obtain permission from the suspect to conduct a search.
2. Apprehend suspect *with* his drug supply. (Constructuve possession is very difficult to prove.) If the drugs are inside a building, apprehend the suspect at his door; then enter the room without forcing the door. (Damage sustained in a police action with regard to property damage subjects the officers to a civil recovery for damages.) If entry must be made to secure drugs, the "no-knock rule" of some states will apply.
3. Lack of subterfuge. Most states do not allow subterfuge, deceit, or trickery to get a suspect to open the door. *If an officer knocks on the door and the suspect asks who it is the officer should reply with his own name.* Many peddlers do not know their clients and will open the door for anyone who leaves him with the impression he is a customer.

Buy Programs for Drug Enforcement

A commonly used technique for drug enforcement is to have an officer or employee pose as a buyer. This is perhaps one of the most effective methods of operation. The buy cases made and the information received on related crimes are invaluable in furnishing leads and supplemental information to field officers. A police operator, with the proper introduction from an informer, can pose as a buyer. For a limited period of time the undercover officer may be able to secure indictments for the sale of drugs on a large number of street peddlers. Occasionally, with proper financial support, the next higher echelon of peddler may be reached.

A weakness of a "buy program" is usually the lack of street informers who will introduce the operator into his circle of peddler friends. A caution to be exercised in purchasing from

How to Conduct a Drug Investigation

drug peddlers is that proper identification of the peddler be made by the undercover operator. Two or three purchases are always desirable from each peddler.

A common method of operation is to seek a large number of secret Grand Jury indictments and serve them at the same time. This procedure utilizes a large number of officers who are familiar with suspects in the area where the purchases are made and who may develop independent cases at that time.

At the state and federal levels "buy programs" of large quantities of drugs are standard procedure. Locally, money to support such a program is rare.

Determination of Drug Type

A field officer frequently encounters situations where he is in doubt about a substance in someone's possession. If a substance is a narcotic drug a preliminary determination may be made by:

1. Observation—the appearance of marihuana, morphine tabs, opium, heroin, and cocaine.
2. A taste or smell test may be made if an opiate containing hydrochloric acid is suspected. A very small bit of heroin on the moistened end of a finger will have a strong, bitter taste and a stinging aftertaste.
3. The smell of burning marihuana may distinguish it from regular tobacco.
4. Microscopic examination of marihuana will distinguish it from oregano or alfalfa hay.
5. Questioning—when suspects attempt to evade ownership of an unknown substance or when they are unwilling to give a credible story for a substance being hidden in vehicle, clothing, etc.
6. Spot-plate tests will not normally be made by the field investigator unless there is ample quantity of the drug. It is usually best to wait for full laboratory tests since illegal synthetics may not respond to spot test chemicals.
7. Commercial packaging—often substances will be purchased or stolen and will be in a familiar container, i.e., codeine, turpin hydrate, Demerol, etc.
8. Admission of ownership—when there is a group involved and there is a probability of a joint possession prosecution, and a possibility that one or more persons may admit to ownership.

Buy Programs for Drug Enforcement

The Enforcement Procedures
for Opium and Its Derivatives

All natural opium and derivatives usually originate outside the United States, and in-transit apprehension is the only way large quantities of this contraband can be seized. The seizure of these drugs is frequently made with interception at a port of entry, through information and follow-up investigations, and incidental contacts of the field officer.

Interceptions

The Federal Bureau of Narcotics and Dangerous Drugs and the Customs Agency Service have prime responsibility for the enforcement of federal drug laws. These agencies, in cooperation with the Bureau of Immigration and Naturalization, maintain an international pressure on drug production and importation. These agencies work with both voluntary and paid informers (see Figure 4.5).

Border check stations coordinate the seizure of sizable quantities of drugs each year. These seizures, while they have an impact upon the flow of drugs, cannot in themselves stop importation. Border patrol units work closely with state and local police in watching for suspects and vehicles suspected of drug smuggling.

Information and Follow-up Investigations

Most local drug cases are the result of this procedure. Word of a pending drug shipment is often circulated to the street peddler so he may obtain the necessary funds to make a purchase. When the street peddler knows about a shipment it is only a matter of time until the prostitutes are contacted for money and this information quickly becomes known to the police. The information about the shipment and the actual shipment frequently coincide so that an officer must activate an immediate investigation. An investigation may progress in the following manner:

1. Information is verified through re-questioning of the original informer. The officer must know:
   Who will have the drug?
   How does he carry the drug?

How to Conduct a Drug Investigation

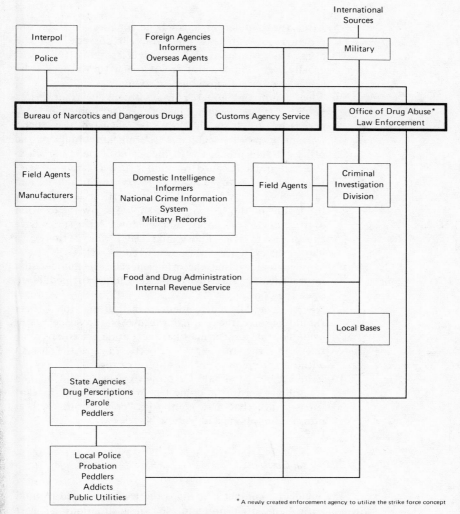

Figure 4.5. Organizational chart and source of information for the federal agencies charged with drug control.

> Who are the street pushers the peddler is most apt to contact?
>
> How does the deal go down?

2. Contact other informers who may know the same peddler and attempt to verify all previous information.
3. Endeavor to verify information by follow-up investigation.
4. Ascertain if probable cause exists to either secure a search warrant if time permits or make an arrest based upon reasonable and probable cause.

Buy Programs for Drug Enforcement

5. After the peddler is located, techniques must be improvised to apprehend him while in possession of the drug. Each situation varies; however, the officer will usually wait and attempt to approach the suspect as he leaves or returns to his house or room.

6. When conducting a search always obtain a warrant if time permits. If the search must be made immediately, a permissive search should always be requested. If neither a warrant has been secured or permission obtained, the officer should proceed with the search if there is reasonable and probable cause to conduct such a search.

7. If an attempt is to be made to seize the contraband and the suspect is inside a building, the officer should know the layout of the structure. He should know the location of the toilet, rear doors, and windows. Most states have exceptions to the "knock and wait" rule if there is a danger the evidence will be destroyed.

8. It is mandatory that the officer develop techniques that do not involve subterfuge or trickery to get the peddler to open the door.

9. As part of his independent investigation, the officer should observe the normal routine of the suspect. For example, the suspect may have a routine for going to the telephone, the store, etc. It is better to seize the suspect without forced entry into his house or room.

10. Evidence seized should be properly labeled and marked for submission to the crime lab. When searching, be alert for evidence that may point to a "connection," such as notations in phone and address books.

Incidental Contacts

The incidental contact is perhaps the least acclaimed method of combating the drug problem. In these situations an alert uniformed officer in the normal course of patrol and the investigation of other crimes will discover narcotics activity. Field officers should be trained in drug recognition and encouraged to take direct action against the violator. Sizable shipments of drugs have been seized by uniformed officers because they were aware of the small suspicious actions of suspects which might indicate drug involvement. When stopping a vehicle for any violation, be sure to watch for furtive movements such as:

1. Concealment of contraband under the dashboard or seat.

2. Dropping or flipping contraband onto the sidewalk or into the gutter.

3. Dropping contraband through a hole in the floor of the vehicle.

4. When approaching the vehicle and contacting the driver, observe these conditions:

   What is the condition of the pupils of the eye?

   Normal size is about 4 mm.

   Contracted, pinpointed, and barely able to see?

   Dilated, about 10 to 16 mm? If the pupil is about normal size or slightly dilated and fixed when exposed to a strong light, it may indicate drug use. Redness surrounds the pupil if marihuana is being used.

5. If the driver appears intoxicated, but does not smell of alcohol, the pupil may be an indicator of the type of drug being used—dilated for most stimulants, contracted for most depressants.

6. A doctor should make the determination as to drug usage if other objective symptoms indicate some type of intoxication.

In his contact with the suspect or other person, an officer should be alert for hypodermic marks. For example, the neck area under the ear, the inner elbow, the back of the hands, and the forearms are common injection sites.

When searching a vehicle for drugs, small quantities of powder, balloons, or other paraphernalia commonly used by drug peddlers should be noted. If there is insufficient probable cause for arrest, a report should be made in writing and forwarded through regular department channels to the drug detail.

Specific laws govern how an investigation is conducted. From your State Codes find the appropriate sections that will enable you to fill in the blanks below.

State Drug Laws

Most states have adopted statutes based upon the Uniform Narcotic Drug Act. The state statutes specify which narcotics are prohibited and which are permitted on prescription. The state statutes have sub-sections which include dangerous drugs that may be acquired on prescription and hallucinogenics which are prohibited from general public use.

Buy Programs for Drug Enforcement

State Law Governing Narcotic Possession. _____

_____

State Law Governing Narcotic Sale. _____

_____

State Law Governing Narcotic Addiction. _____

_____

State Law Governing the Registration of Addicts. _____

_____

State Law Governing the Seizure of Automobiles Used to
Facilitate Narcotic Traffic. _____

_____

State Laws Governing Dangerous Drugs. _____

_____

State Laws Governing Prescriptions. _____

_____

State Laws Governing Psychedelics and Hallucinogenics._____

_____

Handling Crimes Associated with Drug Usage

The ultimate solution to drug abuse must remain with the user. In the past, police restraint and control of the user has been highly restrictive, punitive in nature, and in reality has offered no permanent solution to the drug abuse problem. Today there are a number of alternatives within which the criminal justice system may work in dealing with the user. They are: (1) recognition of addiction and legal processing of the excessive drug user, (2) direct arrest and/or civil commitment, and (3) referral to resident and non-institutional programs for treatment.

Recognition and Processing of the User

There are two philosophies governing narcotic and dangerous drug addiction. The first approaches the drug problem as a sickness. The second is to use criminal detention to isolate the user from society. Police recognize the former method as a better approach to the problem and have moved to use available facilities for medical care and civil commitment of the user. Where care facilities are not operational or available in sufficient quantity the isolation of a user in jail facilities is the only recourse.

History indicates that political manipulation has been instrumental in making drug abuse a social rather than a medical problem.[1] The closure of an unproved clinic system in the 1920s forced the drug user into a situation controlled by organized crime. Once this step had been taken punitive action against the addict became the only control device. Doctors who may have the authority to maintain an addict on drugs have preferred not

[1] Richard Brotman and Alfred Freedman, *A Community Mental Health Approach to Drug Addiction*, (Washington, D.C.: Government Printing Office, 1968), p. 4.

chapter
5

to become involved in the unresolved questions about the narcotics they may prescribe, how often they may prescribe, and how much may be prescribed.[2] Because of these problems, the systematic treatment of drug abusers is still a battle between those who advocate arrest and isolation and those who prefer a clinical and rehabilitation approach.

Law enforcement officers are legally required to enforce existing statutes. Thus it is important for them to understand the basic psychological and sociological traits of the drug abuser.

The following statements give some insight into the attitudes of the addict as to his reason for drug use.[3]

> Studies have shown that the majority of heroin addicts used a milder form of drugs before graduating to heroin
>
> A potential addict generally starts with some type of a dangerous drug, progresses to marihuana, then finally graduates to heroin. This does not illustrate a causal relationship but illustrates how drugs become available to the average user.
>
> In most cases, contrary to opinion, an addict will be introduced to a new drug by a friend or associate, rarely by a peddler.
>
> He advances to the new drug seeking a new thrill or experience.
>
> He almost inevitably likes the results of his experimentation and for this reason continues with the drug until such time as he is introduced to a stronger drug.
>
> Heroin addiction is the end result of his experimentation.
>
> Heroin addiction is a disease of association.
>
> An addict uses heroin primarily because he likes it, he likes what it does to him, and/or how it makes him feel. One author describes this as a manifestation of inadequate, immature, passive, and dependent personality.[4]

After continual use, the user becomes addicted and then must continue with drug use or suffer definite physical withdrawals.

[2]This is an administrative determination made by the government. (Linder Case 1925)

[3]In laymen's terms, these are the prevailing police attitudes used by many departments as guidelines. Furnished courtesy of the Carpenteria Police Department, California.

[4]Glaser and Oleary, *op. cit.,* p. 15.

Handling Crimes Associated with Drug Usage

Soon the addict's body builds a tolerance to the drug and the addict finds it necessary to increase the dosage to receive the desired euphoric effects of the drug.

The police officer, regardless of his personal attitude toward the drug problem, need not look beyond the crime statistics to find a justification for isolating the user.

Certain crimes such as theft, shoplifting, and street robberies may be reduced drastically with the removal of the addict from the street (i.e., after mass arrests coupled with a "buy program," the crimes reported in the downtown area of Los Angeles dropped more than 75 percent immediately following the enforcement action. Crime rates gradually returned to normal after a period of about three weeks).

A federal estimate to sustain a drug habit is $15 to $100 per day. Taking the minimum figure, the addict spends in excess of $5,000 per year on drugs. When converting stolen merchandise into cash it means he must steal in excess of $20,000 per year to maintain a minimum habit.[5]

The money pouring into the business of supplying drugs supports the criminal element on both an individual and organized basis.

To dispense drugs to the user through sponsored clinics has not been successful. One reason may be that the tendency of the user is not to accept a reasonable, sustaining dosage. Most users become "hogs." Other general traits of the user have been identified for the field officer.[6]

What does the addict think about?

The addict lives in a world of his own, a world of drugs. His every thought is of the drug. His only true friends are other addicts. He feels that outsiders don't understand him but look upon him as if a freak.

His primary concern is when and where is he going to get his next fix.

He is constantly thinking of how he is going to finance his next purchase.

He rarely, if ever, displays a genuine desire to rehabilitate, although he may feint a desire for sympathy from judges and members of his family.

[5]Federal Bureau of Narcotics and Drug Abuse, *Fact Sheet, No. 5, op. cit.,* p 5-2.

[6] Courtesy of the Carpenteria Police Department, 1971.

Recognition and Processing of the User

Generally speaking, the addict likes the world he lives in simply because he is impulsive, unstable, and unable to plan ahead.[7]

He gives little thought to sex, food, sleep, and other necessities of life; these are relatively unimportant to him.

General physical appearance of the "hard narcotic" addict.

The depressant narcotics, such as heroin and opium, slow down the body organs. An addict's heart beats slower, therefore, he is always *cold*.

Due to poor blood circulation, an addict's hands will be noticeably cold and clammy.

He will generally appear overdressed. Often, he will wear a sweater or coat during the summer and an overcoat during the winter months.

Upon entering an addict's room, one immediately notices the high room temperature.

Addicts seem to prefer long-sleeved sport shirts as they tend to hide the needle marks on their arms.

He tries not to attract attention with any peculiar or exaggerated dress. He attempts to blend in with the general working class.

Contrary to belief, few addicts will wear dark glasses as they tend to be associated by the general populace with narcotic users. (This trait is more frequently found with users of stimulants.)

His clothing is often soiled and rumpled and might have the appearance of his having slept in them.

Overall appearance.

Addicts rarely bathe, if ever, thereby creating a strong body odor.

Their hair is usually not well kept and generally needs cutting.

Teeth are often stained from lack of cleansing.

Appearance of needle marks.

If right-handed, an addict will generally start his use into his left arm.

Men often attempt to hide their needle marks by injecting into the hairy section of their forearm.

The large veins on the inside of the elbow, along the forearm, and the back of the hands are the most prevalent

---

[7]Brotman and Freedman, *op. cit.,* p. 10. This publication gives a comprehensive insight into the non-medical traits of the addict.

parts of the body used by the addict. These areas are the most accessible large veins in his body that can be easily self-administered.

Continual self-injection in a vein causes the vein to collapse, thereby causing a long scar or "track."

Tracks are indications of previous use only.

Recent use is indicated by a series of small scabs, which under normal conditions last from fourteen to twenty-one days.

Due to the unsanitary conditions under which an addict injects himself a small infection will take place after each injection. Therefore a scab caused by self-injection will last longer than one administered under sterile conditions.

Addicts often will have tatoos placed over the main vein to hide or disguise their needle marks.

Eating habits of the addict.

After addiction the addict gives little attention to a proper diet.

The money he does obtain goes toward the purchase of narcotics, not for food.

He often becomes sick and suffers from malnutrition because the digestive and excretory system does not function with heavy drug usage.

Due to his improper diet and the continued practice of injecting impurities into his blood supply, he is very susceptible to jaundice.

The addict craves sugar.

Due to the constant injection of milk sugar mixed with the heroin in his blood stream, the addict builds up a tolerance to sugar as well as the drug.

He builds up a definite craving for sugar.

When he drinks coffee, it will be generally mixed with three or four spoons of sugar.

Foods that an addict does desire contain a high quantity of sugar, thus creating a milk sugar habit.

There may be moral reasons why the addict should be removed from society. The officer's prime responsibility, however, is to insure the addict a proper diagnosis of his addiction and that the proceedings remain within the framework of the law. Prior to showing the physical signs of addiction, an addict usually shows psychosocial traits.

Who Are the Addicts?

With much debate about addiction and drug dependence, five categories of addicts based upon psychosocial factors are identified here.

1. A person who says he is an addict but in reality belongs to a social group that admires addiction. This person does not typically use a narcotic.
2. A narcotic user with a strong emotional involvement with the person who administers or supplies the drug. The effect of the drug is secondary.
3. A regular narcotic user who develops little tolerance for the drug and may not suffer withdrawals. He uses the drug to relax and is able to sustain a fairly normal life.
4. A person who has physical pain. This person takes narcotics because he thinks he needs them.
5. The person who is the classical addict. His systems demand the narcotic and will develop withdrawal symptoms when they fail to get it.[8]

There are other patterns based upon psychological factors, but these psychosocial patterns are sufficient to illustrate to the field officer the complexity of his contact with drug users. These patterns cannot be used as the basis for arrest, but they should indicate the reactions of people who become involved with drugs.

Diagnosis of Physical Addiction

A field officer is placed in the position of becoming an expert in recognizing the physical symptoms of drug addiction.

When interrogating a narcotics user, the investigator's approach is to tell the user of his illegal use, not to ask. The user will lie, minimize, and attempt to deceive if he thinks the investigator is unfamiliar with the use of narcotics. For this reason, the investigator must know as much as possible about narcotics and their use. If the investigator can impress upon the user extensive knowledge of the subject, the process of examination and interrogation becomes much easier.[9]

Impressing the user does not require telling him all the in-

[8]Adapted from Brotman and Freedman, *op. cit.,* p. 13.

[9]This information is taken from guidelines established for use by the Los Angeles Police Department Narcotic Division.

Handling Crimes Associated with Drug Usage

vestigator knows about narcotics and their use. The impression upon the user of the investigator's extensive knowledge is accomplished by telling the user what the investigator knows about the use of narcotics by the individual being examined.

The following actions performed while making a preliminary examination will indicate to the user that you are making certain mental determinations and will serve to demonstrate your knowledge of the use of narcotics:

1. Examine the veins of the arms carefully.
2. Feel the scar tissue, roll it between the fingers. This will often disclose scabs and punctures not previously noted.
3. Make a close inspection of the scabbed areas.
4. Press raised areas gently, inquire about tenderness. (There may or may not be tenderness.)
5. Point out blue dots over the veins. They are the result of burning a hypodermic needle with a match, supposedly to clean it. After the injection the carbon residue in the needle is deposited under the skin.

Drug addiction is a state of periodic or chronic intoxication produced by the repeated consumption of a drug. Its characteristics include:

1. An overpowering desire or need (compulsion) to continue taking the drug and to obtain it by any means.
2. A tendency to increase the dose.
3. A psychological and generally a physical dependence on the effects of the drug.
4. An effect detrimental to the individual and to society.[10]

There are basically three states of addiction which the enforcement officer may encounter.

Euphoria
    apprehension
    released inhibitions
    susceptibility to suggestion
    exaggerated emotions

Anxiety
    elation
    excitability
    disorientation
    mental confusion

[10]World Health Organization definition.

Antagonism
    suspicion
    hysteria
    grandiose ideas

In handling an addict the officer should know what drug a suspect is using and how large a habit he has. In the preliminary conversation with a suspect the officer should establish rapport. Prior to any examination, review the suspect's history. If the suspect believes his habit is known, he may not attempt lies and deception. The suspect should be asked:

1. Do you fix yourself?
2. What reaction do you get?
3. What time today was your last (or first) fix?
4. How much did you use and how often do you fix?
5. Where did you fix?
6. Do you have a "yen" or feel sick?

The answer to each of these questions is significant with respect to the degree of addiction:

Question 2 indicates whether or not the suspect's body has developed a degree of tolerance.
    Question 4 establishes the frequency of use and may tend to indicate degree of addiction.
    Question 5 establishes that drugs were used. A determination of the suspect's permanent residence may also help. The suspect's use should be within the county to establish venue.

A physical examination of the addict should be conducted to verify his statements.

1. Arms—most frequently used.
2. Examine calves, ankles, thighs, groin, neck, inside lower lip, and on the genitals.
3. While examining and questioning, watch for withdrawal symptoms: yawning, sniffling, nasal drip, perspiration, gooseflesh, chills, and dryness of mouth.
4. Scar tissues will be hard lumps, pink swellings, or bluish-yellow bruises over a vein. Scabbing will occur in about two days and last until about twenty-one days if they are not scrubbed or washed. The following should assist in determining the age of the scab:

Handling Crimes Associated with Drug Usage

Fresh, one to two days—light pinkish orange
Three to four days—orange
Five to ten days—light brown
Ten to fifteen days—brown, slightly raised
Fifteen to twenty-one days—dark brown, slightly raised, with flaking of tissue around scab.

Figure 5.1 shows mark locations commonly noted on the body of an addict.

The following list shows withdrawal symptoms according to severity:

Mild	Moderate	Marked	Severe
Yawning	loss of appetite	deep breathing	vomiting
watering eyes	dilated pupils	fever	diarrhea
running nose	tremor	insomnia	weight loss
sneezing	gooseflesh	restlessness	
perspiration		rise in blood pressure	

Withdrawal symptoms begin eight to fourteen hours after the last dose. In sixteen to eighteen hours, the state is still mild. The addict's condition continues to worsen until seventy-two hours have passed. In five to seven days, acute symptoms have disappeared. Mild withdrawal symptoms are demonstrated for three to four months.

Since heroin is the most common addicting drug diagnosed by the field officer, additional information may be helpful in processing the heroin user. Heroin may be used either hypodermically or sniffed (horned).

Horning Heroin
1. Heroin is used in this manner to avoid prosecution and discovery.
2. By sniffing the heroin into the nose, the drug is absorbed into the blood.
3. Destruction to the nose—heroin eats away the cartilage in the nose until a complete hole is formed from one nasal passage to the other. Scar tissue forms in the mucus membrane and inflames mucus membrane.
4. By horning heroin a person receives only about 35 to 50 percent of the full effect of the narcotic.
5. Heroin is generally horned by beginners who don't want

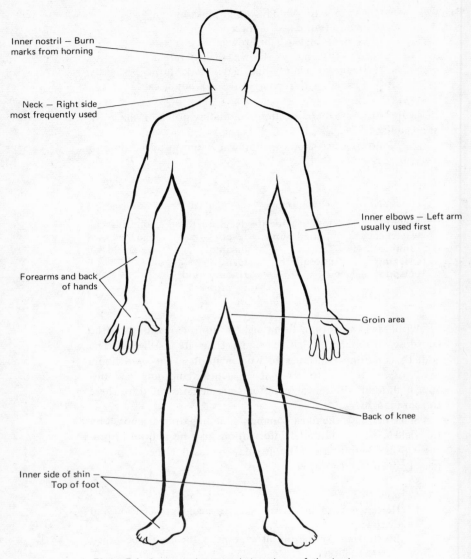

Inner nostril — Burn marks from horning

Neck — Right side most frequently used

Inner elbows — Left arm usually used first

Forearms and back of hands

Groin area

Back of knee

Inner side of shin — Top of foot

Figure 5.1. Common hype-mark locations of the body.

to risk discovery or arrest, or by peddlers who can afford to horn large amounts in order to receive the same feeling as an addict and avoid discovery and arrest.

6. It is almost impossible to prosecute a person who horns a narcotic such as cocaine or heroin because a user who horns does not have good objective symptoms of use.

Handling Crimes Associated with Drug Usage

Nalline is often one method of positively determining usage.

Hypodermic Injection

1. Put the heroin powder in capsules (ten per gram) in a spoon. The amount used will depend upon the degree of addiction.
2. Add water.
3. Cook the solution with a match until the drug dissolves.
4. Draw the solution in bottom of spoon through a small piece of cotton into outfit—this acts as a filter.
5. Inject the drug into a vein.

The full effect of the heroin is gained by injecting directly into the bloodstream. The spinal effect of heroin is gained in this manner and takes one or two minutes to be felt.

Effect on the Body under Heroin Influence

Eyes have pin-point pupils.
Decreased sensibility to pain, hunger.
Slower breathing, general state of lethargy or inactivity.
The nervous system, glands, and all organs have retarded functions.
Spine is stimulated: rubbing or scratching of the nose, face, or body.
Cerebral depressant, causes disorientation to existing conditions.

Effects on Body Not Under the Influence of Heroin (or When Consumption Is Less Than the Tolerance Developed)

Restlessness
Yawning
Running nose
Hoarseness
Gooseflesh
Hot flashes
Chills
Diarrhea

From all indications, narcotics and dangerous drugs constitute a large and expensive problem for not only law enforcement

Recognition and Processing of the User

officers but for society in general. What has not been clearly indicated by statistics is that every community, regardless of its size, is inclined to have drug problems to some degree.

It is estimated that rehabilitation of the addict, if done properly, would cost 150 to 200 million dollars per year.[11] It is, however, possible that part of this cost may be recovered from the manpower gain and recovered taxable income.

Direct Arrest or Civil Commitment

Officers who face the reality of immediate drug enforcement may find that the confinement of a user is the most direct route to the solution of the problems of drug usage. The officer, under most state laws, can make a physical arrest and proceed with criminal prosecution or he may waive criminal proceedings and secure a civil commitment.[12]

The Physical Arrest

Whether the final disposition is criminal or civil, the action is usually initiated by a physical arrest.[13] When a person is discovered to be under the influence of or has acquired a dependence for certain drugs, the officer's only alternative is to make a physical arrest. In making a physical arrest the officer should:

Determine the extent of use by objective symptoms if possible. This may be shown by coordination, physical appearance, etc., as described in section one of this chapter. If there are no hypodermic marks but symptoms indicate addiction or dependence, a doctor should examine the person and give a written opinion as to the extent of use and degree of drug dependence. Establish venue by determining where the ingestion of the drugs took place.

After the physical arrest for drug violations (except sale), the use of civil commitment may be desirable.

[11] Federal Bureau of Narcotics and Drug Abuse, *Fact Sheet, No. 5, op. cit.*

[12] Brotman and Freedman, *op. cit.,* p. 16.

[13] The 1967 Metcalf-Volker Bill. An arrested addict who was not otherwise ineligible could apply for civil commitment in lieu of prosecution. Many, however, found this commitment to be undesirable since they were committed to long periods of parole if they resumed using drugs.

Handling Crimes Associated with Drug Usage

Civil Commitment

With the restrictive role of the United States Narcotic Hospitals, state programs are the most readily available accommodations for the user. Commitments are made by:[14]

1. Voluntary initiative on the part of the addict.
2. Referral by the court as part of a probationary program.
3. Assignment by the court as part of an imposed sentence.

In the civil commitment of the user an officer processes the addict in conformance with the law of his state.

The commitment of an addict either for arrest and physical isolation or for civil commitment and treatment will be based upon the following probable cause:

> When a police officer has reasonable cause to believe that a person is addicted, or,
> Is in imminent danger of becoming addicted, or,
> Petitions the district attorney to have the person taken to a suitable medical institution, or,
> Person may be processed criminally under existing law.[15]

Referral to Other Agencies for Treatment of the User

The officer serves as a referral source for the drug addict and should be familiar with these programs.

Residence Facilities. Examples such as the Daytop Lodge and the Daytop Village in New York City serve paroled violators in residence facilities. The treatment methods are based largely upon the "anticriminal society" of Synanon.[16] The methods are based upon the belief that addicts can most successfully be treated by ex-addicts.

Synanon. This California institution emphasizes a form of group psychotherapy known as "reality" or "attack" therapy and is designed to develop individual self-sufficiency.[17] This program

[14]The criteria for commitments in the various states closely follow "The Narcotic Addict Rehabilitation Act" cited in the Appendix 1.

[15]California Penal Code Section 6500 and Welfare and Institutions Code Section 3102.

[16]Brotman and Freedman, *op. cit.,* p. 7.

[17]*Ibid.*

Direct Arrest or Civil Commitment

gives the user an opportunity to escape the reality of day to day social and economic tension while recovering his psychological balance. He can talk out his problem with other addicts in therapy sessions.

The Dole-Nyswander Outpatient Clinic. The addict has a drug tolerance built up during six weeks of hospitalization and then is given daily high "blocking" dosages of liquid methadone which eliminate the craving for drugs and block the effects of any opiates if they are taken.[18]

The Nalline Program. This program, while not necessarily voluntary, does serve as a possible model for handling large numbers of addicts. It is an outpatient program developed for parolees. The narcotics offender is required to submit to periodic Nalline tests as part of his parole. Nalline will indicate, by pupil reaction, whether the subject is under the influences of any opiate drug. The program's strength lies in deterring the continued use of narcotics and at the same time permit the subjects to work and lead a relatively normal life in a non-institutional, community environment.

Many state and municipal hospitals have developed facilities for voluntary commitment of the addict. In these facilities treatments such as methadone substitution are used.

The use of marihuana has been described more as a drug habituation than as an addiction. Drug habituation is described as a condition resulting from the repeated consumption of a drug which includes these characteristics:

A desire (but not a compulsion) to continue taking the drug for the sense of improved well-being that it engenders.

Little or no tendency to increase the dose.

Some degree of psychic dependence on the effect of the drug, but absence of physical dependence and, hence, no abstinence syndrome.

A detrimental effect, if any, primarily on the individual.[19]

Because of the unpredictable effect of marihuana, there is no set pattern of use symptoms. However, the following are symptoms which are most generally present:

[18]Brotman and Freedman, *op. cit.* This program is questionable and the financing of such programs are being phased out of federally funded projects.

[19]World Health Organization definition.

Handling Crimes Associated with Drug Usage

1. Dilated pupils with slow or no reaction to light.
2. Bloodshot eyes.
3. Rapid speech.
4. Dryness of mouth.
5. Lack of inhibitation—false bravery.
6. Distorted space and time perception (careful and studied movements).
7. Drowsiness and lethargy as terminal effect.

The presence of a *single* symptom is *not* conclusive and could be caused by reasons other than the use of a narcotic. A combination of symptoms should be present.

The Police Role in Drug Education

The public has been bombarded with horror stories about the drug abuser, unsubstantiated claims of massive increases of drug use, and the emergence of sure-fire cures by an increasing number of social scientists. As a result, citizens are saturated with fear, misinformation, and unproductive nonsense about the way in which drug abuse evolves and is controlled. If this misinformation is to be replaced with factual knowledge, law enforcement officers have an important function in education. The education dispensed by law enforcement should basically be restricted to facts concerning their function in the drug abuse programs.

Drug education may be approached in three steps: (1) the field officer as a teacher, (2) basic curriculum areas for officer involvement, and (3) the field officer as a community resource person for drug education.

The Field Enforcement Officer as a Teacher

The field enforcement officer should share in the transmission of information on drugs to the public. The field officer will be participating in drug education for these reasons:

The field officer is in a position to see the end result of excessive drug usage. He can give factual information about the nature of the drug user.

The field officer investigates drug abuses and other crimes and accidents where drugs are involved. He presents first hand information to a listener.

chapter

6

By presenting actual cases and facts, the local field officer may motivate citizens to hold more wholesome attitudes and show more patterns of acceptable behavior.

The practical field knowledge possessed by the officer is helpful in counteracting misconceptions transmitted by intelligent but uninformed persons.

The officer relates to the community when identifying with local problem cases.

The impact of traditional education upon those who become drug users is debatable. Those who eventually become hard-core addicts are generally school dropouts or have extreme difficulty with school subjects and school discipline. Thus, drug education structured into the regular school curriculum does not reach those most prone to drug abuse. Outside instructors such as doctors, policemen, parole and probation officers can frequently reach the marginal student. Based upon this premise it becomes important for the field officer to be prepared to meet with students.

In selecting student audiences the police officer should insist upon fairly mature students above the sixth grade level. Education in the earlier grades (1–6) should be done by a teacher who is specially trained to deal with younger students. An officer should be prepared to present and communicate regarding the drug problem in the following ways:

1. Approach the drug problem from a social and legal viewpoint. Leave the medical, pharmacological and psychological views to doctors or other experts.

2. Do not threaten, preach, or moralize to the audience. Some of the more drug-prone personalities will accept this as a challenge.

3. Emphasize that drug use creates rather than solves problems for the individual and for society. Indicate that drug abuse is only one of many social problems.

4. Stress how the student can be helpful in curbing the drug problem through referral of information to proper authorities.

5. Explain drug laws and the rationale for making many drug violations a felony (i.e., the process of search and seizure) even though a defendant may ultimately be found guilty of only a misdemeanor.

6. Allow for discussion time so that any misinformation may be cleared up.

7. Omit emotionalism from your presentations. This type of information may do more damage than good. The officer

The Field Enforcement Officer as a Teacher

need only relate known facts and figures in attempting to clarify student misinformation.

Basic Curriculum Areas for Officer Involvement

The President's Crime Commission recommended that the National Institute of Mental Health be a clearinghouse for drug information. However, there was no plan included for getting this information to schools and interested public groups. Logically, the parent and the school teacher should transmit basic information about drugs to a child. Only when these sources fail to reach the child should a social agency such as a law enforcement agency become involved.

Law enforcement agencies have historically and properly been the last resort for assuming educational responsibility. When, however, no other social agency can fill the void in drug education, it then becomes a responsibility of law enforcement to fill that void. In the past, law enforcement agencies have assumed the responsibility of drug education programs without a documented program. The area and the expertise for drug education has been based primarily upon the individual efforts of an officer within an agency. The presentation by this individual then was based upon his own philosophy of what should be told about drugs rather than upon an educationally sound program.

Drug education by law enforcement officers extends far beyond the basics outlined here. If an officer is to be involved in drug education he should gain information about the various drugs from such academic courses as chemistry, biology, psychology, and sociology. If an officer is to engage in drug education, he should have an understanding of the related implications of drug abuse and the complex nature of the cure. Because few officers have this background, law enforcement efforts in drug education has been subject to much criticism.

If law enforcement is to retain a proper role in drug education, and there are many areas in which only law officers have the expert knowledge to present factual information, an outline should be developed for the officers involved. This could be a first step toward the development of an effective program.

An educational program by a law enforcement officer dealing with drugs has two objectives: first, to prevent the development of excessive drug use; and second, to apprehend the drug user and peddler once drug abuse is discovered.

In suggesting a curriculum for the field officer it is important to consider the individual policies of different police departments which in most cases reflect the attitude of the community toward the drug problem. Many communities take a pragmatic approach and do nothing about drug education. These communities take action against drug abusers in only the most flagrant cases and then without publicity and fanfare. Other communities respond in the opposite way by acting on all cases with fanfare and maximum publicity.

Drug education programs tend to follow these enforcement philosophies. The philosophy of a community, whichever course it may follow, is entitled to educational materials that are valid and accurate to a reasonable degree. The following curriculum suggestions are adaptable to the trend a community chooses to take.

Suggested Discussion Topics for the Field Officer

Most experts in the field of drug education establish breaks in the subject matter to be presented at grades 6, 10, and 13. Since an officer is generally not prepared to present materials to students below the sixth grade level the emphasis here is upon the more mature student above the sixth grade.

The Grades 7–10

A student is very impressionable at this age, and the officer's role should be restricted to such topics as:

1. Assist the student to understand his legal rights and responsibilities.
2. Explain how the student shares the same responsibility as the officer in drug control.
3. Impress upon the student that drugs are not bad, it is only the abuse of the drugs that create a problem.
4. Show how drugs have influenced history. Illustrate not only some of the benefits of drugs to mankind, but also the dangers and detriments.
5. Explain the laws regarding prescriptions and why this type of control is necessary.

6. Explain in a simplified way how search and seizure laws work and why illegal drug traffic is difficult to control.
7. Illustrate why drug users talk to policemen. Show why he is a willing informer.

With the limited time an officer has to address an audience he should make a strong attempt to illustrate the areas that will best explain the legal and procedural problems regarding drugs. Let the school teacher, the chemist, and the doctor tell the student about the composition, classification, and effects of drugs.

Students Above the Tenth Grade

To this group of students and to the general public, an officer will be able to talk about all issues. At this age a person will have formed fairly definite values about drugs. Suggested topics for presentation to this age group may include the following:

1. Illustrate how laws are legal commands for an officer to take action and explain how search and seizure laws regulate enforcement action.
2. Cite pertinent empirical research results regarding an addict's personality patterns and why rehabilitation is so difficult to obtain.
3. Impress upon the student that he must assume the burden of self-identity in rejecting drugs.
4. Show how contacts and relationships are established between users and nonusers.
5. Document how drug use is directly and indirectly related to other crimes.
6. Stress the importance of having citizen cooperation in drug control activity.

Conclusion

This material has not attempted to be comprehensive in presenting all the complexities of the drug problem. The problem is too vast and the causes of use are too intricate to be discussed fully. A field officer is not expected to fully understand the pharmacology, the behavioral effects, and the full sociological impact of drugs in order to take the necessary legal action in his contacts with law violators. He should, however, know legal methodology and techniques of investigation in order to present a complete, legal case to the court.

The field officer is an important part of an evolving system which attempts to cope with drug abuse more adequately. History has shown that law enforcement alone has very little impact upon the spread of drug usage. Thus, it is important that the drug enforcement officer views himself as a part of a more comprehensive system. No one is yet certain what combinations of prevention, enforcement, and rehabilitation are most desirable for a workable system. The field officer must be an active participant in developing policy to insure that proper combinations are applied to a workable drug program.

Conclusion

Glossary
of
Terms

ADDICTION

In 1957, the World Health Organization (WHO) defined drug addiction as a state of periodic or chronic intoxication produced by the repeated consumption of a drug. Its characteristics include: (1) an overpowering desire or need (compulsion) to continue taking the drug and to obtain it by any means, (2) a tendency to increase the dose, (3) a psychic (psychological) and a general physical dependence on the effects of the drug, and (4) an effect detrimental to the individual and to society.

CENTRAL NERVOUS SYSTEM

The brain and spinal cord.

CONVULSIONS

An involuntary and violent irregular series of muscular contractions.

DELIRIUM

A condition characterized by mental excitement, confusion, disordered speech, and often hallucinations.

DEPRESSANT

Any of several drugs which sedate by acting on the central nervous system. Medical uses include the treatment of anxiety, tension, and high blood pressure.

DRUG DEPENDENCE

As described in 1963 by WHO, drug dependence is a "state arising from repeated administration of a drug on a periodic or continuous basis." Its characteristics will vary with the agent involved. This is made clear by designating the particular type of drug dependence in each specific case—for example, drug dependence of the morphine type, of the cocaine type, of the *Cannabis* type, of the barbiturate type.

HABITUATION

As defined in 1957 by WHO, drug habituation is a condition resulting from the repeated consumption of a drug, which includes these characteristics: (1) a desire (but not a compulsion) to continue taking the drug for the sense of improved well-being that it engenders, (2) little or no tendency to increase the dose, (3) some degree of psychic dependence on the effect of the drug, but an absence of physical dependence and, hence, no abstinence syndrome, and (4) a detrimental effect, if any, primarily on the individual.

HALLUCINOGEN
Any of several drugs, popularly called psychedelics, which produce sensations such as distortions of time, space, sound, color, and other bizarre effects. While they are pharmacologically non-narcotic, some drugs (e.g., *Cannabis*) are regulated under federal laws.

HYPNOTIC
An agent that induces sleep.

NARCOTIC
This term has two definitions. Medically, a narcotic is any drug that produces sleep or stupor and also relieves pain. Legally, the term means any drug regulated under national or international narcotic laws. Some of these regulated drugs are pharmacologically non-narcotic (e.g., cocaine).

PHYSICAL DEPENDENCE
Physiological adaptation of the body to the presence of a drug. In effect, the body develops a continuing need for the drug. Once such dependence has been established, the body reacts with predictable symptoms if the drug is abruptly withdrawn. The nature and severity of withdrawal symptoms depend on the drug being used and the daily dosage level attained.

POTENTIATION
Potentiation occurs when the combined action of two or more drugs is greater than the sum of the effects of each drug taken alone. Potentiation can be very useful in certain medical procedures. For example, physicians can induce and maintain a specific degree of anesthesia with a small amount of the primary anesthetic by using another drug to potentiate the primary anesthetic. Potentiation may also be dangerous. For example, barbiturates and many tranquilizers potentiate the depressant effects of alcohol.

PSYCHOLOGICAL DEPENDENCE
An attachment to drug use which arises from a drug's ability to satisfy some emotional need of an individual. This attachment does not require a physical dependence, although physical dependence may seem to reinforce psychological dependence. An individual may also be psychologically dependent on substances other than drugs.

Glossary of Terms

PSYCHOSIS

A major mental disorder; any serious mental derangement. "Psychosis" replaces the old term "insanity."

SEDATIVE

An agent which quiets or calms activity and tends to promote sleep.

SIDE-EFFECTS

A given drug may have many actions on the body. It is given specifically for one or two of the more prominent actions. The others, usually irregular effects, are called side-effects. They are not necessarily harmful, but may be annoying.

STIMULANT

Any of several drugs which act on the central nervous system, producing excitation, alertness, and wakefulness. Medical use include the treatment of mild depressive states, overweight, and narcolepsy—a disease characterized by an almost overwhelming desire to sleep.

TOLERANCE

With many drugs, a person must keep increasing the dosage to maintain the same effect. This characteristic is called tolerance. Tolerance develops with the barbiturates, with amphetamine and related compounds, and with opiates.

TOXIC EFFECTS (POISONING)

Any drug taken in excessive amounts can act as a poison. The margin between the dosage that produces beneficial effects and dosage that produces toxic or poisonous effects varies greatly. Moreover, this margin will vary with the person taking the drug.

TOXITUDE

A condition caused by the habitual absorption of a harmful substance by an individual either by necessity or in order to satisfy a more or less marked need; or for pleasure whether or not the user is aware of the disadvantages or dangers he incurs, or to which he exposes others.

Comprehensive Drug Abuse Prevention and Control Act of 1970

This bill is a comprehensive document providing for: (1) authority for increased efforts in drug abuse prevention and rehabilitation of users, (2) more effective means for law enforcement aspects of drug abuse prevention and control, and (3) overall balanced scheme of criminal penalties for offenses involving drugs. A summary of the act follows.

Title I: Rehabilitation

The bill provides authority for the Department of Health, Education, and Welfare to increase its efforts in the rehabilitation, treatment, and prevention of drug abuse, through community mental health centers and through public health service hospitals and facilities.

Over a three-year period 75 million dollars in increased authorizations are provided for community mental health center facilities to deal with narcotic addicts and drug dependent persons, 29 million dollars is authorized for drug abuse education activities, and 60 million dollars is authorized for special facilities in areas having high percentages of narcotic addicts and drug dependent persons.

Increased research and training activities are authorized through the National Institute of Mental Health out of appropriations otherwise authorized for that institute. Section 4 of the bill would encourage treatment of narcotic addicts by individual physicians.

appendix

Title II: Control and Enforcement

The bill provides for control by the Justice Department of problems related to drug abuse through registration of manufacturers, wholesalers, retailers, and all others in the legitimate distribution chain, and makes transactions outside the legitimate distribution chain illegal.

The drugs with respect to which these controls were enforced initially are those listed in the bill. These drugs are those which by law or regulation have been placed under the control under existing law. This includes all hard narcotics and opiates, marihuana, all hallucinogens (such as LSD), amphetamines, barbiturates, and tranquilizers subject to abuse.

A procedure is established for classification of future drugs which may create abuse problems. Under this procedure, if the Attorney General feels that a drug should be controlled, he will gather data and request a scientific and medical evaluation by the Secretary of HEW. If the Secretary, on the basis of these and any other data, determines that the drug should not be controlled, the Attorney General may not control the drug; otherwise, the Attorney General may publish notice in the Federal Register and proceed in accordance with procedures which provide notice and opportunity for a hearing to list the drug for control.

An exception is made in the case of treaty obligations of the United States. If a drug is required to be controlled pursuant to an international treaty, convention, or protocol in effect on the enactment of the bill, the drug will be controlled in conformity with the treaty or other international obligations.

In the case of drugs providing serious addiction or abuse problems (those listed in Table Four) tighter controls are provided. These controls include the establishment of quotas for imports and for domestic manufacture. Transfers of these drugs may only be made through the use of officially prescribed order forms, with a copy furnished to the Attorney General.

All persons in the distribution chain are required to be registered, and, with certain exceptions, must keep records with respect to all transfers of controlled drugs. Practicing physicians are required to keep records of schedule I substances; keep records of narcotic drugs in other schedules which they dispense (as distinguished from prescribing or administering) to patients; and if they charge for other controlled drugs regularly, keep records of these transactions. Researchers are not required to keep records with respect to controlled substances used by them

Comprehensive Drug Abuse Prevention and Control Act of 1970

at registered establishments, as long as the establishment keeps records.

Criminal Penalties

The bill revises the entire structure of criminal penalties involving controlled drugs by providing a consistent method of treatment of all persons accused of violations. With one exception involving continuing criminal enterprises, all mandatory minimum sentences hereafter discussed are eliminated.

Possession of controlled drugs is made a misdemeanor, except where the possession is for the purpose of distribution to others. In the case of the first offense of simple possession, the court may place the offender on probation for not more than one year. If at the end of the period of probation the offender has not violated the conditions of probation, the proceedings against him may be dismissed without a court adjudication of guilt.

If the offender is under twenty-one when the offense occurs, he may obtain a court order expunging from all official records all mention of his arrest, indictment, trial, and finding of guilt. The procedure described above for first offenders may only be utilized once by an individual, and a second offense of possession thereafter will be treated as a first offense.

Manufacture or distribution of illicit drugs is punishable by up to fifteen years in prison in the case of schedule I or II narcotic drugs, and by up to five years in the case of non-narcotic schedule I or II drugs or any other controlled drugs in schedule III. Illegal sales or manufacture of schedule IV drugs (generally minor tranquilizers) would carry a three-year sentence for a first offense of schedule V drugs would carry a one-year sentence.

Second offenses carry double the penalty for first offenses.

Where a person over eighteen sells drugs to a person under twenty-one, the first offense punishment is twice that otherwise prescribed.

Where an individual engages in a continuing criminal enterprise involving a continuing series of violations undertaken by him in concert with five or more other persons and from which he derives substantial income, he is punished by a mandatory minimum sentence of not less than 10 years and up to life imprisonment, together with a fine of up to $100,000 and forfeiture to the United States of all profits derived from the enterprise.

Control and Enforcement

Administration

The bill specifies a number of administrative authorities for the Attorney General, authorizing research and educational programs relating to the law enforcement aspects of drug abuse, cooperation with state and local law enforcement authorities, administrative inspections, forfeitures, and execution of search warrants—including authority to enter premises without giving notice of authority and purpose if a judge or United States magistrate has authorized such entry in the warrant after determining that there is probable cause to believe that:

1. Property sought may and, if notice is given, will be easily and quickly destroyed or disposed of, or
2. The giving of such notice will immediately endanger the life or safety of the executing officer or another person.

Commission on Marihuana and Drug Abuse

The bill establishes a Presidential commission on marihuana and drug abuse which will study and report to the Congress within one year on problems involved in marihuana use, and within two years on the causes of drug abuse and their relative significance.

Title III: Imports and Exports

Title III of the bill as recommended by the Committee on Ways and Means provides for control of imports and exports of drugs subject to abuse through a system of registration of importers and exporters, and permits for or notification to the Attorney General of transactions, with criminal penalties for transactions outside the legitimate distribution chain.

Total Authorization

The bill authorizes $403 million in additional appropriations as follows:

1. Increased authorization for community mental health centers: 1971, $10 million; 1972, $25 million; 1973, $40 million.
2. Drug abuse education: 1971, $20 million; 1972, $10 million; 1973, $12 million.

Comprehensive Drug Abuse Prevention and Control Act of 1970

3. Special projects: 1971, $20 million; 1972, $20 million; 1973, $20 million.
4. Commission on marihuana and drug abuse: $1 million.
5. Department of Justice: 1972, $60 million; 1973, $70 million; 1974, $90 million, plus an additional amount for increased enforcement personnel of $6 million per fiscal year.

Control Provisions

The bill is designed to meet problems that have arisen under existing narcotic and dangerous drug laws due to recent governmental reorganization, court rulings, and the changing posture of the drug problem facing this country.

Since 1914 the Congress has enacted more than fifty pieces of legislation relating to control and diversion from legitimate channels of those drugs referred to as narcotics and dangerous drugs. This plethora of legislation has necessarily given rise to a confusing and often duplicative approach to control of the legitimate industry and to enforcement against the illicit drug traffic. This bill collects and conforms these diverse laws in one piece of legislation based upon new scientific information, the restructured federal law enforcement efforts under Reorganization Plan No. 1 of 1968, and greater information concerning the scope of the problem. The bill classified substances subject to control in five schedules according to their abuse potential and psychological and physical effects. It sets forth penalties which are designed to correspond to violations involving substances contained in the respective schedules.

The bill is designed to improve the administration and regulation of the manufacturing, distribution, and dispensing of controlled substances by providing for a "closed" system of drug distribution for legitimate handlers of such drugs. Such a closed system should significantly reduce the widespread diversion of these drugs from legitimate channels into the illicit market, while at the same time providing the legitimate drug industry with a unified approach to narcotic and dangerous drug control.

The bill also specifically recognizes our international obligations under the Single Convention of 1961 and will allow the United States to immediately control under the schedules of the bill drugs hereafter included under schedules of the Single Convention upon the recommendation of the World Health Organization.

Existing Federal Laws Governing Drugs: PL91-513 (1970)

Part D: Offenses and Penalties

Section 401. Prohibited Acts: A—Penalties

Section 401(a). This section makes it unlawful for a person to knowingly or intentionally (1) manufacture, distribute, dispense, or possess with intent to manufacture, distribute, or dispense, a controlled substance, except as authorized by this title; or (2) create, distribute, dispense, or possess with intent to distribute or dispense, a counterfeit substance.

Except in the case of violations punishable under section 405 (relating to distribution to persons under 21), *section 401(b)* establishes the following penalties for anyone who violates section 401(a):

(1) (a) In the case of a narcotic drug in schedule I or II, up to 15 years in prison and/or a fine of not more than $25,000 may be imposed, except that if the person has one or more prior convictions for an offense punishable under this subsection, or for a felony under another provision of this title or of title III or other law of the United States relating to narcotic drugs, marihuana, or depressant or stimulant substances, such person shall be sentenced to not more than 30 years and/or a fine of not more than $50,000. A special parole term of 3 years is imposed in addition to any prison term under this paragraph, and if there exists a prior conviction, the special parole term is for 6 years.

(b) In the case of schedule I or II non-narcotic substance or a schedule III substance, a violator shall be imprisoned for not more than 5 years and/or fined not more than $15,000, except that in the case of prior convictions as above described, the punishment is not more than 10 years and/or a fine of not more

appendix

than $30,000. A special parole term of 2 years is added to the prison term unless there was a prior conviction, in which case it would be for 4 years.

(2) In the case of a schedule IV substance, the sentence is to be for not more than 3 years and/or a fine of not more than $10,000. If there is a prior conviction as above described, the sentence shall be for not more than 6 years and/or a fine of not more than $20,000. A special parole term of 1 year is imposed except in the case where there is a prior conviction, in which case it would be for 2 years.

(3) In the case of a schedule V substance, sentence is to be for a prison term of not more than 1 year and/or a fine of not more than $5,000. If there is a prior conviction, the punishment shall be for not more than 2 years and/or a fine of not more than $10,000.

Section 401(c) provides that the special parole term imposed under this section or section 405 may be revoked if its conditions are violated, and in such a case the original term of imprisonment is increased by the period of the special parole term. The prisoner may be required to serve part or all of the new prison term. The special parole term is in addition to and not in lieu of any other parole provided by law.

Section 402. Prohibited Acts: B—Penalties

Section 402(a) makes it unlawful (1) to distribute or dispense a controlled substance which is a prescription drug without a lawful prescription in violation of section 309, (2) for a registrant to distribute or dispense a controlled substance not authorized by his registration to another registrant or other authorized person, or to manufacture a controlled substance not authorized by his registration, (3) for a registrant to distribute a controlled substance without the required identifying symbol or without its container being securely sealed where required, (4) to remove, alter, or obliterate a required symbol or label, (5) to refuse or fail to make, keep, or furnish any record, report, notification, declaration, order or order form, statement, invoice, or information required by this title or title III, (6) to refuse entry into any premises or inspection authorized by this title, (7) to remove, break, injure, or deface a seal placed upon controlled substances pursuant to this act, or to remove or dispose of substances so placed under seal, or (8) to use for his own advantage or reveal, other than to duly authorized officers or employees of the United States or to the courts (including disclosure pursuant to discovery process), any information acquired in the course of an inspection authorized by this title concerning any method of process which as a trade secret is entitled to protection.

Section 402(b) prohibits a person who is registered to manufacture any schedule I or II controlled substance which is (1) not expressly authorized by his registration and by a properly assigned quota, or (2) in excess of a quota assigned to him.

Section 402(c) (1) subjects a violator of this section to a civil penalty of not more than $25,000, except as 402(c)(2) provides otherwise. The United States district court or otherwise proper United States court having jurisdiction of matters of this nature shall have jurisdiction to enforce this paragraph. Section 402(c)(2)(A) provides that in the event of prosecution by information or indictment alleging that the violation was committed knowingly, and if the trier of fact so finds, such person shall, except as provided by section 402(c)(2)(B), be imprisoned for not more than 1 year and/or fined not more than $25,000. Section 402(c)(2)(B) provides that for a violation referred to in subparagraph (A) committed after one or more prior convictions, the violator shall be sentenced to a term of imprisonment of not more than 2 years and/or fined not more than $50,000. Section 402(c)(3) provides that except under the conditions specified in 402(c)(2), a violation of this section does not constitute a crime, and a judgment and the imposition of a civil penalty shall not give rise to any disability or legal disadvantage based on conviction for a criminal offense.

Section 403. Prohibited Acts: C—Penalties

Section 403(a) makes it unlawful for any person to knowingly or intentionally (1) in the case of a registrant, distribute controlled substances in schedule I or II in the course of his legitimate business, except pursuant to an order form issued by the Attorney General, (2) use fictitious, revoked, or suspended registration numbers, or a number issued to another person, in connection with manufacture or distribution of controlled substances, (3) acquire a controlled substance by misrepresentation, fraud, forgery, deception, or subterfuge, (4) furnish false, fraudulent, or incomplete material information in any application, report, record, or other document required under this law, or (5) make, distribute, or possess an instrument designed to print or reproduce the trademark or other identifying mark of another upon any drug or container or its labeling so as to render such drug a counterfeit substance.

Section 403(b) makes it unlawful for any person to knowingly or intentionally use any communication facility in committing or facilitating the commission of a felony under this title or title III. Each separate use of a communication facility is deemed a separate offense, and the term "communication facility" is defined as any instrument for the transmission of writing, signs, signals, pictures, or sounds.

Section 403(c) provides that any person who violates this section shall be imprisoned for not more than 5 years and/or fined $30,000. If there is a prior conviction, the person shall be imprisoned for more than 10 years and/or fined not more than $10,000.

Section 404. Penalty for Simple Possession; Conditional Discharge and Expunging of Records for First Offense

Section 404(a) makes it unlawful for any person knowingly or intentionally to possess a controlled substance unless it was obtained from a practitioner directly or pursuant to a valid prescription or order, except as otherwise authorized by this title or title III. Any person who violates this section shall be imprisoned for not more than 1 year and/or fined not more than $5,000. If there is a prior conviction under this subsection, he shall be sentenced to not more than 2 years and/or fined not more than $10,000.

Section 404(b)(1) provides that if a person, who has not previously been convicted of violating subsection (a) of this section, any other provision of this title, or any other law of the United States relating to narcotic drugs, marihuana, or depressant or stimulant substances, is found guilty of violating section 404(a), after a trial or a plea of guilty, the court may, without entering a judgment of guilty, and with the consent of such person, defer further proceedings and place the person on probation upon such reasonable conditions as it may require and for such a period, not to exceed 1 year, as the court may prescribe. Upon a violation of a condition of probation, the court may enter an adjudication of guilt and proceed as otherwise provided. The court may dismiss the proceedings against such person and discharge him from probation before the expiration of the probation period. If the person does not violate the conditions of probation, the court may discharge the person and dismiss the charges against him at the end of his term of probation. Such discharge and dismissal shall be without a court adjudication of guilt, but a nonpublic record shall be retained by the Department of Justice solely to be used by the courts in determining whether or not, in subsequent proceedings, such person qualifies under this subsection. A discharge and dismissal shall not be deemed a conviction of a crime, but may occur only once with respect to any person.

Section 404(b)(2) provides that after a dismissal and discharge under the above subsection, if the person was not over 21 years of age at the time of the offense, he may apply to the court for an order to expunge from all official records (other than the nonpublic records retained by the Department of Justice) all recordation of his arrest, indictment or information, trial, finding of guilty, and dismissal and discharge pursuant to this section. The court shall make such an order if the person fits the qualifications and the order shall restore such person, in the contemplation of the law, to the status he occupied before such arrest, indictment, or information. No person as to whom such order has been entered shall thereafter be held guilty of perjury or giving a false statement by reason of his failure to recite or acknowledge such arrest, indictment, information, or trial in response to any inquiry.

The committee is confident that judges, in administering the provisions of this section, will recognize that many defendants coming before them will be in need of medical treatment and that the judges will require that these persons undergo some form of prescribed treatment as a condition of their probation.

Section 405. Distribution to Persons Under Age 21

Section 405(a) provides that anyone at least 18 years of age who violates section 401(a)(1) by distributing a controlled substance to a person under the age of 21 may be punished by twice the amount of imprisonment and/or fine, and twice the special parole term, authorized in section 401(b) for that substance. Thus, in the case of a first offense under this section, imprisonment of up to 30 years, or a fine of up to $50,000, could be imposed, plus at least 6 years of special parole, if a schedule I or II narcotic is involved; 10 years of imprisonment, a $30,000 fine, or both, plus 4 years of special parole, if a non-narcotic schedule I or II substance or any schedule III substance is involved; 6 years of imprisonment, a $20,000 fine, plus 2 years of special parole in the case of a schedule IV substance; and 2 years of imprisonment, a $10,000 fine, or both, in the case of a schedule V substance.

Section 405(b) provides that if a person commits a violation of section 405(a) after a prior conviction under this section (or of section 303(b)(2) of the Federal Food, Drug, and Cosmetic Act as in effect prior to enactment of this bill, which relates to distribution to minors), the prison term and/or fine will be up to three times the corresponding penalty and special parole term under section 401(b). Thus in the case of a second or subsequent offense under this section, these sentences could range from up to 45 years of imprisonment or $75,000, plus 9 years of special parole, for a narcotic schedule I or II substance; to 15 years of imprisonment or $45,000, plus 6 years of special parole, for a non-narcotic schedule I or II substance or any schedule III substance; to 9 years of imprisonment or $30,000, plus 3 years of special parole, in the case of a schedule IV substance; and to 3 years of imprisonment or $15,000, or both, in the case of schedule V substances.

Section 406. Attempt and Conspiracy

Section 406 provides that any person who attempts or conspires to commit any offense defined in this title may be punished by imprisonment and/or fine which may not exceed the maximum amount set for the offense, the commission of which was the object of the attempt or conspiracy.

Section 408. Continuing Criminal Enterprises

Section 408 provides that persons engaged in continuing criminal enterprises involving violations of this bill, from which substantial profits are derived, shall, upon conviction, be sentenced to not less than 10 years in prison, and may be imprisoned up to life, with a fine of up to $100,000, plus forfeiture of all profits obtained in that enterprise. A second conviction under this section will lead to a mandatory sentence of not less than 20 years and up to life imprisonment, a fine up to $200,000, and forfeiture of all such profits.

References

Alpert, Richard, and S. Cohen. *LSD.* New York: New American Library, 1966.

Ausubel, David P. *Drug Addiction: Physiological, Psychological and Sociological Aspects.* New York: Random House, 1958.

Beckman, H. *Dilemmas in Drug Therapy.* Philadelphia: Saunders, 1965.

Bloomquist, Edward R. *Marihuana.* Beverly Hills: Glencoe Press, 1968.

Blum, Richard. *Utopiates; The Use and Users of LSD-25.* New York: Atherton Press, 1964.

Brotman, Richard, and Alfred Freedman. *A Community Mental Health Approach to Drug Addiction.* Washington, D.C.: Government Printing Office, 1968.

Ciba Foundation Study Group. *Hashish: Its Chemistry and Pharmacology.* Boston: Little, Brown, 1965.

Cohen, Sidney. *The Beyond Within; the LSD Story.* 2d ed. New York: Atheneum, 1967.

Cutting, W.C. *Handbook of Pharmacology: the Action and Uses of Drugs.* 3rd ed. New York: Appleton-Century-Crofts, 1967.

Drug Abuse: Escape to Nowhere; A Guide for Educators. Philadelphia: Smith, Kline and French Laboratories in cooperation with the National Education Association, NEA, 1967.

Finlator, J. "Drug abuse control: operations of BDAC agents," *FDA Papers I,* Washington, D.C.: Government Printing Office, pp. 4-8, April 1967.

Hoffer, Abram, and H. Osmond. *The Hallucinogens.* New York: Academic Press, 1967.

Hyde, Margaret O. *Mind Drugs.* New York: McGraw-Hill, 1968.

Kalant, O.J. *The Amphetamines: Toxicity and Addiction.* Springfield, Ill.: Charles C. Thomas, Publisher, 1966.

LaBarre, W. *The Peyote Cult,* Hamden, Connecticut: Shoe String Press, 1964.

Lauri, Peter. *Drugs: Medical, Psychological and Social Facts.* New York: Penguin Books, 1967.

Leake, Chauncey D. *The Amphetamines, Their Actions and Uses.* Springfield, Ill.: Charles C. Thomas, Publisher, 1958.

Louria, Donald B. *The Drug Scene.* New York: McGraw-Hill, 1968.

Maurer, David W., and V. Vogel. *Narcotics and Narcotic Addiction.* 3rd ed., Springfield, Ill.: Charles C. Thomas, Publisher, 1967.

O'Donnell, John A., and John C. Ball, eds. *Narcotic Addiction.* New York: Harper & Row, 1966.

Solomon, David, ed. *LSD: The Consciousness-Expanding Drug.* New York: Putnam's, 1964.

Surface, William. *The Poisoned Ivy.* New York: Coward-McCann, 1968.

Time, Inc. *The Drug Takers: A Special Report,* New York: Time-Life, Inc., 1965.

U.S., Department of Defense. *Drug Abuse: Game Without Winners, A Basic Handbook for Commanders.* Washington, D.C.: Government Printing Office, 1968.

U.S., President's Commission on Law Enforcement and Administration of Justice. *Task Force Report: Narcotic and Drug Abuse.* Washington, D.C.: Government Printing Office, 1967.

Williams, John B., ed. *Narcotics and Hallucinogens*— A Handbook. rev. ed., Beverly Hills, Calif.: Glencoe Press, 1968.

Films
on
Drug
Abuse

Bennies and Goofballs. National Medical Audiovisual Center, Chamblee, Georgia 30005 (B&W: 20 min.).

Beyond LSD. BFA Educational Media, 2211 Michigan Ave, Santa Monica, California (Color: 25 min.).

Bureau of Narcotics and Dangerous Drugs on the uses of marihuana, LSD and "pills" (B&W: 15 min.).

Drug Addiction. Encyclopedia Britannica Films, 38 West 32nd Street, New York, New York 10017 (B&W: 20 min.).

Drugs: Facts Everyone Needs to Know. Fiorelli Films Inc., Stamford, Connecticut (Color: 29 min.).

Drugs and the Nervous System. Churchill Films, 662 N. Robertson, Los Angeles, California 90069 (Color: 20 min.).

Drugs and the Nervous System. Churchill Films, 662 N. Robertson, Los Angeles, California 90069 (B&W: 22 min.).

Fight or Flight. IACP, 1319 18th Street N.W., Washington, D.C. (Color: 16 min.).

Forests of the Night. Association Instructional Materials, 600 Madison Ave., New York, New York. (Color: 15 min.).

Hide and Seek. Center for Mass Communication of Columbia University Press, 440 West 110th Street, New York, New York 10025 (B&W: 15 min.).

Hooked. Churchill Films, 662 N. Robertson, Los Angeles, California 90069 (B&W: 25 min.).

Keep Off The Grass. Sid Davis Productions, 1046 S. Robertson, Los Angeles, California 90035 (Color: 20 min.).

LSD-25. Professional Arts, Inc., P.O. Box 8484, Universal City, California, 91608 (B&W: 25 min.).

LSD. Audiovisual Branch, United States Navy, Pentagon, Washington, D.C. (B&W: 30 min.).

LSD: Insight or Insanity. Bailey Films, 6509 DeLongpre Avenue, Hollywood, California 90028 (Color: 20 min.).

LSD: Trip or Trap. Sid Davis Productions, 1046 S. Robertson, Los Angeles, California (Color: 20 min.).

Marijuana. Bailey Films, 6509 DeLongpre Avenue, Hollywood, California 90028 (B&W: 25 min.).

Marijuana: The Great Escape. BFA Educational Media, 2211 Michigan Ave., Santa Monica, California (Color: 20 min.).

Mind Benders. National Medical Audiovisual Center, Chamblee, Georgia 30005 (B&W: 25 min.).

Narcosis. California Peace Officers Association, 802 Forum Building, Sacramento, California (B&W: 24 min.).

Narcotics: A Challenge. The Narcotic Educational Foundation of America, 5055 Sunset Boulevard, Los Angeles, California 90027 (B&W: 25 min.).

Narcotics—The Inside Story. Charles Cahill and Associates, Inc., P.O. Box 3220, Hollywood, California 90028 (Color: 15 min.).

Narcotics—Why Not. Charles Cahill and Associates, Inc., P.O. Box 3220 Hollywood, California 90028 (Color: 15 min.).

Seduction of the Innocent. Sid Davis Productions, 1046 S. Robertson, Los Angeles, California 90035 (B&W: 10 min.).i,

The Addicted. Association Films, Inc., 600 Grand Avenue, Ridgefield, New Jersey 07657 (B&W: 50 min.—2 parts).

The Agents of Drug Abuse. Penelope Films Inc., 1440 Clay, San Francisco, California 94019 (Color: 38 min.).

Tea, Horse and Crime. Audio Visual Center, Indiana University, Bloomington, Indiana (Color: 24 min.).

The Dangerous Drugs. The Narcotic Educational Foundation of America, 5055 Sunset Boulevard, Los Angeles, California 90027 (B&W: 20 min.).

The Losers. Carousel Films, Inc., 1501 Broadway, New York, New York, 10036 (B&W: 30 min.).

The Pill Poppers. Sid Davis Productions, 1046 S. Robertson, Los Angeles, California 90035 (Color, no time given).

The Riddle. Public Affairs, Office of Economic Opportunity, 1200-19th Street, N.W., Washington, D.C. 20506 (B&W: 30 min.).

The Seekers. State of New York Narcotic Addiction Control Commission, Albany, New York, 12203 (B&W: 30 min.).

Way Out. Valley Forge Films, Inc., Chester Springs, Pennsylvania 19425 (B&W: 105 min.—2 parts).

For further information on these and other films you may contact the producing company, the public library, your local university film service, or local military bases.

Films on Drug Abuse

Drug Abuse Audio–Visual Media

DCA Educational Products. 4865 Stenton Ave., Philadelphia, Pa. Two sets of color transparencies. The first set consists of 22 units on "How Safe Are Our Drugs," at $54.75. The second set consists of 20 units on "The Use and Misuse of Drugs," at $59.75. Complete set, $114.50.

Lockheed Information Systems. Box 504, Sunnyvale, California. A 15-hour course of instruction aimed at junior and senior high school students entitled, "Drug Decision," consisting of a three-hour movie-animation segment produced by Warner Brothers; 300-page student response and decision manual; five-hour teacher preparation and data file.

National Drug Abuse Clearing House, Box 1080, Washington, D.C.
Has comprehensive file on studies and publications. Write for information.

Raytheon Learning Systems Company. 457 S. Dean Street, Englewood, New Jersey.
Set of ten filmstrips on drugs, each with record, teacher's guide, and pad of 50 score sheets for student participation. Series covers: "Barbiturates and Amphetamines," "Marijuana," "LSD," and "Teenagers and Drugs." Complete set $250.00.

School Health Education Study (3M Company). Box 3100, 3M Center, St. Paul, Minnesota.
A comprehensive health education program. Set of four books in four grade levels from kindergarten through 12th grades, plus teacher-student resource on "Use of Substances that Modify Mood and Behavior" set $10.00 from 3M Education Press, Box 3344, St. Paul MN 55101. Four sets of color transparencies, each containing 20 visuals for Level I (kindergarten through 3rd grades); four sets for Level 2 (4th through 6th grades); and five sets for Level 3 (7th through 9th grades), and six sets for Level 4 (10th through 12th grades). $33.00 per set.

Texas Alcohol Narcotics Education, Inc., 2814 Oak Lawn Ave., Dallas, Texas.
Filmstrip with 33 1/3 rpm record and booklet on each of five subjects: "Alcohol: Fun or Folly," "Smoking. . .or Health,"

"Glue Sniffing: Big Trouble in a Tube," "LSD: Trip or Trap" and "Why Not Marijuana."

The Robert J. Brady Co., 130 Que St. N.W., Washington, D.C. 20002.

Transparencies and slides for training academies and for public information programs. Send for information.

Winston Products for Education. P.O. Box 12219, San Diego, California.

Comprehensive packages on drug abuse. Send for information.